THE WILL TO LIVE

The story of a remarkable and heroic woman who in a few short weeks after the Japanese invasion of Malaya was twice shipwrecked; the second occasion resulting in her spending four days on a raft without food or water under a tropical sun. Picked up by a Japanese destroyer near death, she then endured three and a half years starvation and hard labour, in Japanese hands. Her will to live pulled her through and after the war she returned to nursing and became Matron-in-Chief of the Royal Army Nursing Corps and a Dame of the British Empire.

BRIGADIER THE RIGHT HON.
SIR JOHN SMYTH, Bt., V.C., M.C.

THE WILL TO LIVE

*The Story of
Dame Margot Turner
D.B.E., R.R.C.*

**With a foreword by
Brigadier Barbara Gordon,
R.R.C., Q.H.N.S.
Matron-in-Chief and Director
Army Nursing Service**

Complete and Unabridged

ULVERSCROFT
Leicester

First published in Great Britain in 1970 by
Cassell Ltd.,
London

First Large Print Edition
published December 1986

British Library CIP Data

Smyth, *Sir* John
The will to live: the story of Dame
Margot Turner, D.B.E., R.R.C..—Large print ed.
1. Turner, Margot   2. Nurses—England
—Biography
Ulverscroft large print series: non-fiction
I. Title
610.73′092′4   RT37.T/

ISBN 0-7089-1560-4

Published by
F. A. Thorpe (Publishing) Ltd.
Anstey, Leicestershire
Set by Rowland Phototypesetting Ltd.
Bury St. Edmunds, Suffolk
Printed and bound in Great Britain by
T. J. Press (Padstow) Ltd., Padstow, Cornwall

Foreword

by *Brigadier Barbara Gordon, RRC,
QHNS Matron-in-Chief and Director
Army Nursing Service*

I AM very grateful to Sir John for inviting me to write a short foreword for this book, which is essentially about my predecessor as Matron-in-Chief QARANC.

For over twenty years Margot Turner's name, and the living proof of her sufferings and her survival of such appalling experiences, has been a byword amongst the QAs. Very few of us, even her closest associates, ever knew the full details; we certainly never heard of them from her.

"Four days alone on a raft"—"Six months' confinement in the cell of a Sumatra jail"—and yet here she was amongst us and had finally risen to the highest position in the Corps.

I repeat, we never heard her story from

her, and it was not until she had retired that I eventually persuaded her to agree to having her experiences written into a book—not for any glory to herself but for the interest it would undoubtedly prove to the Corps. Margot was adamant that the book must be about the experiences and hardships suffered by all those Nursing Sisters and wives who were caught up in the horrors of those events which we call the Fall of Singapore. The joy and privilege of knowing Margot is for her modesty and her matter-of-fact acceptance that she did no more than hundreds of others did, or would have done in similar circumstances.

The deeds of valour and self-sacrifice performed by nurses, forerunners of the modern QAs, in the Crimea, are spoken of with pride when we trace the birth of nursing in this country and in the Army. Is it too fanciful to ask that the heroism, self-sacrifice and devotion to duty of the Army Nursing Sisters in the Far East should be held in just as high esteem? And that Singapore should rank with Scutari when we consider the traditions of the Army Nursing Services?

In making inquiries regarding numbers of QAs involved in the Fall of Singapore I had access to a file referred to later in this book. To read this was a most moving experience and the contents, for sheer pathos and human interest, could in itself be the subject of a book. It is sufficient in this context to say that of the total number of Army Nursing Sisters on the strength of hospitals in Hong Kong, Malaya and Singapore, when these countries were over-run by the Japanese, half either perished at sea or survived only to become prisoners of war. Of those who survived the years of privation less than ten were physically fit to continue in the Service. Margot, in spite of her experiences, was one of these few.

I know this book will be of great interest to Nursing Sisters of Britain and Australia who lived through these years, and to Margot's many friends. And although the events will be history to modern QAs I would commend it most strongly to them and to all those interested in the art of survival.

BARBARA GORDON

Acknowledgements

FIRST and foremost my warmest thanks are due to Dame Margot Turner herself for inviting me to write her very thrilling and inspiring life story and for providing me with all the information I required. She has given me in note form, in speech and in recorded talks, the details of her own life and of her wartime ordeals—and those of some of the other people who shared them with her.

There is a great comradeship amongst ex-prisoners of the Japanese, both male and female, and particularly amongst the Nursing Sisters of all nationalities. They all had to endure one basic hardship in the callousness, and often the brutality, of their Japanese jailers—and many other hardships which arose in consequence.

Margot's own description of events is so clear and vivid that I have often quoted her own words. She is such a modest person, however, and so singularly free of any sense of rancour against the Japanese, that sometimes it might seem as if her own narrative tends to play down the grimness of her sufferings and the courage and steadfastness which enabled her to surmount them. Truth is not only stranger than fiction but often more dramatic and Margot's story needs no embellishment.

With regard to the aftermath of the Singapore surrender in February 1942, I had the benefit not only of Margot's own detailed account, but those of others who shared these ordeals with her. I am extremely indebted to Denis Russell-Roberts and his publishers, The Times Press—Anthony Gibbs and Phillips Ltd, for giving me full permission to make use of his excellent book, *Spotlight on Singapore*, which is one of the classics of that period of the war in Malaya and Singapore. I found it particularly valuable with regard to the escape of "the little ships" from Singapore and the disasters which overtook so many of their passengers.

Spotlight on Singapore, which was published in 1965, begins with these words: "It is true to say that Jackie Smyth has been urging me to write this book since the end of 1945. Now that the book is finished, this is my opportunity to say how grateful I am to him for being the driving force behind my efforts and for giving me at all times his friendly advice and encouragement." I also wrote the foreword to his book.

I am most grateful to Australian Nursing Sister, Betty Jeffrey—who, with the gallant band of Australian nurses, shared Margot's ordeals in the prison camps—for her helpful letters and kindly good wishes for the success of this book; and to Vivian Bullwinkel, now Matron of Fairfield Hospital, Victoria.

My warmest thanks are due to Stoker E. A. Lloyd, RN, for his graphic description of the ghastly massacre on the Banka Island beach, of which he, with Australian Nursing Sister Vivian Bullwinkel and an American civilian, William H. McDougall, were the only three survivors.

For assistance and advice—particularly with the post-war part of the book—for reading the whole manuscript for me, and for writing the foreword, I wish to record my most sincere thanks to Brigadier Barbara Gordon, RRC, QHNS, who succeeded

Dame Margot as Matron-in-Chief and Director of the Army Nursing Service. Brigadier Gordon took me on a visit to her intensely interesting QARANC Training Centre at Aldershot, which I particularly valued, and also all the attention and help I received there from the Commandant, Colonel H. C. Thayer, RRC, the Chief Instructor and 2nd-in-Command, Lieut.-Colonel M. Gara, RRC, and the Curator of the Museum, Mrs. D. Riddlestone.

In addition I would like to record my thanks to the many people who have written to me, or come to talk to me, about Margot. Amongst these I would mention particularly Miss Netta Smith, her close friend in Muntok Camp; Major-General M. H. P. Sayers, OBE, MD, Royal Army Medical Corps; Lieut.-General Sir Harold Knott, KCB, OBE, MA, MD, LLD; Mrs. J. Scorer; Mrs. D. E. Tattersall; Mrs. N. L. Dodd; Dr. Margaret Thompson; Miss Gwen Dowling; Lieut.-Colonel M. K. Thomson; Mrs. R. Sutton; Lieut.-Colonel A. M. Hey, MBE, RRC; Mrs. R. G. Davies; Mrs. Ferguson and Colonel A. Flanagan, MBE; Mr. Ted Le Blanc Smith; Brigadier C. M. Marsden, CBE, MB,

FRCS; and Mrs. Gilmour.

I am grateful to the Editor of the Journal of the Royal Army Medical College Millbank for permission to quote from the January 1960 number. I am much beholden to the Director of the Australian War Memorial Canberra and to Mr. D. F. Mayne, Head of the Photographic Section Imperial War Museum, for their invaluable help over the provision of photos. As always, my old friend, Mr. D. W. King, OBE, FLA, the Chief Librarian of the Ministry of Defence Library (Central and Army), and his staff, have been of enormous assistance in selecting and providing the books I required.

And last but by no means least I give my heartfelt thanks to my invaluable secretary, Miss Jean Gomme-Duncan, MBE, for all her help; and to my wife, Frances, who has not only typed and checked the manuscript, but has acted, as always, as my Editor-in-Chief.

JACKIE SMYTH

Preface

WHEN all resistance ceased in Malaya and Singapore on 15 February 1942, some one hundred thousand British and Commonwealth soldiers went into captivity, of whom ten thousand were to die from the brutal treatment of their Japanese captors; and, in addition, large numbers of British men, women and children from Hong Kong and Malaya were interned—many of the latter having first been sunk or captured at sea on various small vessels and interned on Banka Island, Sumatra and other neighbouring places.

All prisoners and internees of the Japanese suffered mental and physical tortures which were, to say the least of it, intimidating and exhausting. For all of them, men and women alike, there was the constant humiliation of having to stand to attention and bow when confronting even a private soldier of the superior race. Failure to do so would inevitably lead to a blow across the face with a fist or a rifle butt—and any retaliation meant severe punishment or even death. Very few of the senior British officers escaped physical beatings-up on the slightest provocation—and this included the one-armed General, "Piggy" Heath, whose life was greatly shortened by the brutalities he endured. In addition there was a complete absence of news from home, which was almost the greatest hardship, both for the POWs and for their relatives. And the Red Cross parcels were received only by the Japanese; the prisoners practically never had the benefit of these life-giving comforts.

Starvation was the greatest weapon of the Japanese and the threat of a reduction in the meagre ration was a fearful thing. The bestial Kempei Tai, or secret police, were always eager to subject anyone to months of solitary confinement—from which many of their victims never recovered. One who did was the Rt. Rev. J. L. Wilson, KCMG, later to become the Bishop of Birmingham, who was unmercifully tortured over a long period when he was Bishop of Singapore.

In the women's camps, as I have shown in this book, the Japanese went out of their way to inflict the greatest possible hardships on their helpless prisoners; but the courage and spirit shown by the latter were beyond all praise. I have been closely concerned with the cause of the Far Eastern Prisoners of War because I so nearly became one myself and so many of my men were captured in the first Burma Campaign of 1942.

Very little news of the fate of our prisoners of the Japanese was forthcoming until, in 1944, Mr. Anthony Eden (later Lord Avon), then Foreign Secretary, made a very grave pronouncement in the House of Commons as to what had been happening to them. This came as a great shock to the civilized world. Later, in 1944, the Secretary of State for War gave another report regarding the dreadful conditions under which our military prisoners of war were being forced to work on the notorious Burma-Siam railway, generally known as "The Railway of Death". But there was very little information regarding conditions in the civilian internment camps. The QAs of course were really military personnel but the Japanese always refused to regard them as such.

When the war ended I became one of the

original members of the British ex-Prisoners of War Association. Later I became the chairman of a Committee in the House of Commons which put down a motion on the Order Paper to claim compensation from the Japanese "for the brutalities, indignities, and gross under-nourishment to which our British prisoners were subjected". Amazing support was received for this motion from every side of the House of Commons and eventually 297 backbench members signed it; and it also had support from the front benches of both Government and Opposition.

When I rose in the House to move the motion on 10 May 1951 the gallery was full of supporting FEPOWs. I asked for a sum of ten million pounds from the Japanese. Speakers from all sides of the House supported me and the motion was accepted with enthusiasm without a division. As a result two clauses were put into the Peace Treaty authorizing us to take Japanese assets frozen in Great Britain and to have a share in Japanese assets frozen in ex-enemy and neutral countries.

In the next year I became Parliamentary Secretary to the Ministry of Pensions and, amongst my other duties, became responsible for implementing the provisions of the Peace Treaty in so far as these applied to British FEPOWs. It was a colossal job and entailed the establishment of a new section in the Ministry. At first I was told that the sum we should obtain was negligible; but we had many kind and pertinaceous people helping us, Ministers such as Selwyn Lloyd and John Boyd-Carpenter, and the FEPOW Federation itself gave immense assistance. Little by little the frozen assets started to melt.

Eventually, after years of endeavour, we obtained a total of just under £5,000,000. The bulk of this was distributed to individual FEPOWs in *per capita* grants. But with the last quarter of a million pounds John Boyd-Carpenter, the Minister of Pensions and National Security, set up an FEPOW Trust, with myself as the first Government Trustee; and this has been of immense assistance to FEPOWs in need of help. I was honoured to be made, first an honorary FEPOW, and then Honorary Vice-President of the Federation.

In all these matters I worked in the closest touch with General Percival, the President of the FEPOW Federation, and his Committee. We found that a large number of FEPOWs were still suffering from the various tropical bugs and diseases which they had picked up in the prison camps. At that time I was a Governor of Roehampton Hospital, which was also one of the Ministry of Pensions' hospitals. With the warm co-operation of the doctors we had a large tropical diseases ward established in the hospital which all FEPOWs were encouraged to visit for examination and treatment—and thousands did—and many continue to have regular check-ups there.

The FEPOW Federation—under the Presidency, first of General Percival and then, on his death, of Brigadier Phil Toosey —has become one of the strongest and most united ex-Service Associations in the country. Every year they have an inspiring reunion at the Festival Hall where, on Saturday 12 October 1968, they welcomed as a member and Guest of the Evening, Dame Margot Turner.

It was because of my great interest in the prisoners of war of the Japanese that I was particularly pleased at being asked to write this book. Anyone who has been a prisoner of the Japanese is part of one big fellowship, whether they were soldiers or civilians, men or women.

This book, which tells the story of Margot and her fellow sufferers, is a saga of inspiring courage. One hears a great deal of the will to win—and that is indeed a praiseworthy quality. But the will to live is something which comes when the will to win has ceased to have any meaning; when the body has been weakened by malnutrition, ill-treatment and disease; when "England's far and honour a name". Facing up to this situation and facing up to living again when the weary and debilitating years of captivity have ended—that is what this book is all about.

Introduction

A Note on the Evolution of the QARANC

THE Army Nursing Service began on 21 October 1854 when Florence Nightingale took her band of forty nurses to the Crimea. Previous to this, though matrons, head nurses and nurses had been employed to nurse the sick in military hospitals, they were not trained nurses but generally soldiers' wives. Florence Nightingale retired when the Crimean War came to an end and never again assumed an official position in the Army or in a hospital. But she lived for another fifty years and her influence on the development of the Nursing Service was tremendous.

The wounded from the Crimea were brought to Chatham, which was the first hospital to have Sisters on its staff. During the next few years they began working also in military hospitals in London,

Netley and Woolwich.

In 1881 the Army Nursing Service was inaugurated and, in 1889, it was decided that Sisters were to be employed in all military hospitals with a hundred or more beds. The following year marked the beginning of overseas work for Sisters in military hospitals in peacetime and Sisters were sent to Malta, Gibraltar and the Curragh (Ireland), besides being employed in Aldershot, Gosport, Portsmouth, Devonport, Dover, Shorncliffe and Canterbury.

When the South African War started in 1899 the indispensability of the Nursing Service was recognized and a total of fourteen hundred nurses was sent to the battle zone, eighty of whom were supplied by Canada, Australia and New Zealand. On 27 March 1902, at the end of the South African War, the Army Nursing Service, which up to this time had been a civilian body attached to the Army for nursing purposes, ended its existence and became the Queen Alexandra's Imperial Military Nursing Service, with Queen Alexandra as its first President. The 27th March is always celebrated as "QA Day" by QAs all over the world.

The Service was under the immediate control of Her Majesty; she took a keen personal interest in all its affairs and could often be seen in the wards of Queen Alexandra's Military Hospital Millbank. The new grey dress of the QAs, with the distinctive scarlet cape, became famous in military hospitals and garrisons. At the same time a QAIMNS was formed in India on the insistence of Lord Roberts, who was then Commander-in-Chief.

When the First World War started there were only three hundred nurses in the QAIMNS. However, there was an immediate and rapid expansion and, during 1914, 2,223 trained nurses were enrolled and of these 1,803 were sent abroad. By 1919 the Service and its Reserve numbered 10,404 fully trained nurses. The QAs rendered an inestimable service to the Army and to Britain in that very grim struggle, in which the British Army suffered by far the greatest casualties in its history. The nurses' casualties amounted to 36 killed or drowned through enemy action, while 159 died on active service.

In 1926 the QAIMNS in India amalgamated with the QAIMNS at home and the following year the QA Military Families Nursing Service, which had been formed in 1921 to look after Army wives and children, also came into the one Service. So that today a Sister has great scope and variety in her work. Whether in peace or war Sisters had to be prepared to be sent to any station, at home or abroad.

The Territorial Army Nursing Service was founded in 1908, for the purpose of maintaining an establishment of nurses willing to serve in general hospitals in the event of mobilization of the Territorial Army. Its original establishment of 2,117 was increased during the First World War to 7,117, of whom 2,280 served in hospitals overseas. In 1939 the Territorial Army Nursing Service became an integral part of QAIMNS and served with it thereafter in all theatres of war.

In the Second World War the strength of the Nursing Service rose from 624 to over 12,000 and the reputation of the QAs soared to its greatest height. They gave distinguished service in every theatre of war in which British troops were engaged, on the battle fronts, in base hospitals, hospital ships and field hospitals of every sort. Many of them suffered hardships and 220 of them died. In the Second World War their battle casualties were more numerous than in the First because the nurses were farther forward in the battle area. But fatal casualties from disease were fewer because of better control and treatment.

In 1943 the QAs were granted Wartime Commissions with military rank and from then on wore the insignia of their rank. The titles used were the old ATS ones and were varied several times. Field-Marshal Montgomery, at one of his briefing conferences, said: "The most important people in the Army are the Nursing Sisters and the Padres—the Sisters because they tell the men they matter to us—and the Padres because they tell the men they matter to God—and it is the men who matter."

The Nation's memorial to those many nurses who gave their devoted service to the sick and wounded lies in the esteem of the armies in which they served and the eternal gratitude of the men, so many of whom owed their lives to the courage and skill of the QAs.

In 1948 Queen Mary became Commandant-in-Chief of the QAIMNS and, on

1 February 1949, the Service changed its title to the Queen Alexandra's Royal Army Nursing Corps—entirely responsible for its own recruitment and training. In 1950 the Nursing Officers were given the same rank titles as those of the male officers of the Regular Army, the Matron-in-Chief having the top-ranking of Brigadier. QARANC Junior ranks were also taken in to the Corps.

On 17 October 1967 Her Royal Highness Princess Margaret, Countess of Snowdon, Colonel-in-Chief of the QARANC, opened the new Training Centre of the Corps, which stands on the site of the old Royal Pavilion at Aldershot, which had been built in 1856 for Queen Victoria. This very important milestone in the history of the Nursing Service took place during the tour of office of the Matron-in-Chief, Dame Margot Turner, about whose life this book is written.

I have been privileged to know Dame Margot, and her successor, Brigadier Barbara Gordon. Any women's service, military or civil, would be fortunate indeed to have one of these women to lead them —let alone two. Both are very dedicated people—but also fine human beings who quite obviously have had the affection and trust of their officers and nurses—and they certainly have my own sincere admiration.

Throughout my military service I have always had the highest opinion of the QAs who "followed the drum" in war and in peace and set such a wonderful example of service and courage. Florence Nightingale lit the torch when she went the rounds with her fabulous lamp in the hospitals of the Crimea. The Nursing Sisters of today have picked up the torch and, in the last world war, carried it much farther forward on the battlefields than Miss Nightingale ever envisaged. In the years 1939–45, in the ambulance trains and advanced dressing stations the presence of a Sister and a Doctor gave unbelievable comfort to the wounded—and in many cases made just that difference between certain death and a chance to live.

The high standards demanded of a QA were not attained without hard training and a considerable amount of self-sacrifice and self-discipline. It is because I believe that leaders like Dame Margot Turner and Brigadier Barbara Gordon understand the necessity for these qualities that I feel confident that the QARANC of today will remain second to none in the Nursing

Services of the world and continue to fulfil all the high traditions of its history in the years to come.

1

How It All Began

ON the bosom of the Java Sea a small raft drifted helplessly, swept this way and that by strong currents, an infinitesimal speck in the lonely emptiness of the ocean. On the raft lay a woman in the last stages of physical and mental exhaustion, burnt black by the sun and almost at the end of her tether. This was Margot Turner, one of the Queen Alexandra's Nursing Sisters who had been evacuated from Singapore in the dark days of February 1942. How did she come to be there? This is her story.

Margot Turner was born in Finchley on 10 May 1910. Her father, Thomas Frederick Turner, died when she was thirteen and her mother, Molly Cecilia, later married a Mr. Ralph Saw, a most charming man. Margot had three brothers, two older than herself—Dudley and Trevor—and one younger—Peter. Her father worked in a solicitor's office. The Turners lived comfortably and were a very happy family. Margot went to the Finchley County School. This part of her life passed so uneventfully that now she can recall little of it. Later her parents moved to Hampstead.

Margot had always been interested in people, and this was an important factor when she had to decide how she was to earn her living. She couldn't bear the thought of working in an office; but she had met some people in the nursing profession and she eventually decided that this was where she would like to make her life. Her mother warmly supported her decision and started to write round to some of the training hospitals. Margot herself, however, was keen to train at a London hospital and decided that she would try to get into St. Bartholomew's. This was one of the oldest of the teaching hospitals, to which it was most difficult to gain entry. She was just twenty-one when she presented herself for an interview. And it was then that she met Nancy Mitton (later Mrs. R. Sutton) and Jenny Kemsley (later Mrs. J. Scorer) and the three of them struck up a close and lasting friendship.

All three girls were accepted for training

and were sent for six weeks to the Training School off Goswell Road in the City, together with about twenty other probationers, of whom only ten finally came through. They then went to Bart's for three months, at the end of which time they had to pass their big hurdle for final selection. This was certainly an ordeal, with the Chairman of the Governors and the Matron, Miss Helen Day, doing the interviewing. There were two doors to the interview room; the successful probationers left by one door and the failures went through the other door and were not seen in the hospital again.

The nursing profession in those days was a very hard one; discipline was strict, the hours long—6.30 a.m. to 8 p.m. with one day off a month and bad pay—but of course money went a lot farther then and accommodation and food were entirely free. The five hundred nurses lived in the Nurses Home and, despite everything, they managed to have a lot of fun. There were good facilities for tennis and swimming and the London theatres used to send them complimentary tickets.

Nancy, Jenny and Margot shared their grumbles, their achievements and their disappointments; and, between coming off duty at 8 p.m. and lights out at 10.30 p.m., they would generally forgather to brew cocoa, talk interminably and laugh together. They took their holidays together too.

Some of the people who knew Margot at that time have summed up her appearance and her character as: "a big, handsome girl with a 'good' face, wavy hair and very fine eyes. She had a great sense of humour and loved all outdoor things. She was a strong swimmer and a good tennis and hockey player. Physically she was very tough. She was forthright and honest and a true friend. She was also a very strong character and, in those days, deeply religious. She was dedicated to her profession and tackled each job that came along with all her might." Jenny Scorer writes that "Margot took everything in her stride, treating indescribable septic hands and feet, abscesses and ulcers (in the days before penicillin) with a cheerfulness that encouraged both the patients and those who worked with her".

After her four years' training at Bart's Margot took her final hospital exams, but stayed on for another six months to get theatre experience as she had become particularly interested in theatre work. She was then asked to stay on for a further six months. But it so happened that Nancy had taken her on a weekend leave to visit her elder sister, Eleanor, who was a QA (Army Nurse) at Woolwich and was about to depart for service overseas. Margot became intrigued with the idea of becoming a QA herself; she liked the uniform, particularly the smart red capes. So she refused the extension at Bart's and applied to join the QAs.

Unfortunately, because of illness, which kept her out of work for six months, she didn't join the QAs until February 1937, when she was posted to the Cambridge Military Hospital at Aldershot.

At the Cambridge Margot made friends with Dorothy "Jimmy" James (later Mrs. D. E. Tattersall), whom she was destined to meet up with again in India, and Kathleen Thomson. The latter writes:

We spent many happy afternoons together, when off duty, riding through the lanes around Aldershot on derelict bicycles (mine cost five shillings second-hand, and Margot's was little better), playing tennis at Gun Hill House and riding over the plain on horses lent to us by the Gunners.

The highlight of the year was the Aldershot Tattoo, which we Sisters attended on duty. We had a private box and wore our indoor uniforms with white kid gloves. No one ever asked us to do any nursing duty there so we were left in peace to enjoy the show.

Later we were both posted overseas. I had a letter from Margot a week before I became a POW in Hong Kong. I often thought about her during my captivity and wondered what was happening to her. She was such a vital person and had such wonderful spirit that I felt sure she must be still alive somewhere.

On my release in 1945 I at once wrote to the War Office for news of her and was so delighted to learn that she had survived. We met, for the first time for nearly ten years, at the QA Reunion in London in 1946 and how we enjoyed being together again.

In those early days anyone who joined the QAs was on probation for six months and then, if found suitable, was gazetted and received a bronze medal to wear on her cape, which signified that she was a Staff Nurse.

Just before Christmas 1937 Margot was posted to Millbank hospital. She was very upset about this as she was so happy at Aldershot and had made many friends there. In consequence, to start with, she disliked Millbank. But, after a couple of months, she came to like it very much and enjoyed being back in London again. The Sisters lived in the hospital and had a Mess of their own. Margot was now doing general nursing and did not go back to theatre work until she went overseas.

At that time the Sisters did much longer spells of night duty than they do today. At Millbank Margot did a spell which lasted over three months. But she found that, after a bit, she got used to it. During the day the Sisters on night duty had special rooms on the top floor which were quiet and restful. The theatres were always particularly kind to Nursing Sisters and, as at Bart's, the Sisters at Millbank got as many theatre tickets as they wanted.

Behind the hospital was a tennis court, though rather an indifferent one, so Margot preferred to go to Knightsbridge Barracks and ride the Life Guards' horses in the riding school. However, someone objected to this and Margot and her friends went instead to a riding school in Richmond Park, where they enjoyed riding in the fresh air but found their mounts rather small after the Life Guards' horses.

Margot was still at Millbank in 1938 but she wished to be posted overseas. Her great friend, "Jimmy" James, had embarked for India on the *Neuralia* from Southampton in March 1938 and Margot went down there to see her off. At that time the largest number of Army nurses posted overseas went to India, though some went to Egypt. There was a set trooping season, either from September to December or from January to March. In those peacetime days the hot weather months were out so far as trooping was concerned. Sisters were not allowed to apply to go abroad—they just had to go where they were sent. However, in September 1938, Margot got posting orders for India. She was ordered to embark on 5 November on the *Neuralia*.

For Margot, and other QAs who sailed with her, the voyage to India, though of great interest and excitement for anyone who had not experienced it before, was no picnic. There were only three QAs, but many families aboard and they had to work very hard looking after the sick. The voyage from Southampton to Karachi took three weeks and they called at Gibraltar, Malta, Port Said and Aden, being allowed time off to land at each port of call. They arrived in Karachi on 26 November 1938.

The three QAs were posted to different stations—Margot to Bareilly—but they were all three to travel in one compartment together as far as Lahore. Margot, who was always very interested in people, was thrilled with Karachi, its colourful crowds and beautiful setting, and the never-ending hum and chatter of the vast, milling throng in the bazaars. And she revelled in the warm sun after the chills of an English autumn. At that time of year the climate of Karachi was like a perfect English summer and the three QAs in their white topis, red capes and long, white tricoline dresses, felt very over-dressed and found the topis a great nuisance.

They were invited to spend the day at the British Military Hospital; and then, with their bedding rolls—an inevitable concomitant of Indian travel—and their modest amount of luggage, they entrained in a roomy ladies' compartment, being careful to obey the instructions to lock themselves in at night. In those days air-conditioning of railway carriages was by no means commonplace, and the flyproof grids on the windows did little to prevent grit and dust entering the compartment. Crossing the Sind Desert was particularly unpleasant, and the heat too was fierce. But once they had crossed the desert the temperature began to improve and by the time they reached Lahore—where they parted company—the climate was once more temperate. At Lahore Margot changed trains and went on to Bareilly, in the United Provinces, which was less than two hundred miles from Meerut—that historic place where the Indian Mutiny began in 1857.

There were two types of Military Hospital in India at that time, British and Indian. The hospital to which Margot was posted was a British one for British troops and their families and for the British officers and families of Indian Army units. It had a Matron and six QAs, who had their own living quarters and Mess a short distance away from the hospital.

Bareilly was a pleasant little station from many points of view. Margot's first impressions of it were of winter roses and beautiful colourings. The climate in the winter season was superb, glorious sunshine in the daytime but not too hot; a little rain usually fell about Christmas and the evenings were cold enough for fires from November to January; the mornings were fresh and invigorating and many people used to go riding before their day's work began. In this climate everything grew. In the United Provinces for the most part there was plenty of water and in the cold season the grass was green and the gardens gay with every sort of flower—sweet peas mingled with cannas and zinnias, roses bloomed profusely and there were strawberries and plenty of fresh vegetables.

Each of the Sisters had one large living-room and they all fed together in the Sisters' Mess. Life in India just before the Second World War was certainly very enjoyable for the British garrison—and not least for the Nursing Sisters. They worked hard and played hard; everyone was very nice to them

11

and there were plenty of young men who were only too eager to take them to dances and picnics and to lend them ponies and motor cars. And Margot was as popular with the men as she was with her fellow QAs. She was particularly keen to continue with her theatre work, in which she had specialized at Bart's, and she found that if she took a short Army course she would be given specialist work in the theatre, which had the added advantage of bringing her a little extra pay.

A typical day for Margot at the hospital would be a ride at 6 a.m., followed by a bath and breakfast; then duty in the hospital all morning; lunch and a little rest in the afternoon; and in the evening tennis and a swim at the Club, followed perhaps by a film or dance, or just a quiet dinner in the Mess. In the hot weather, when the British battalions and families moved up into the hill station of Ranikhet, leaving perhaps one company in Bareilly, only three Sisters remained in the hospital; the others went up to the hospital in Ranikhet.

Lieut.-Colonel (later Major-General) M. H. P. Sayers, who was acting Commanding Officer of the hospital at Bareilly, recollects Margot as follows:

Margot came from Bart's and I from St. Thomas's, which created a common bond between us and she soon became a friend of mine and of my family. I have the happiest recollections of entertaining her at our old pre-mutiny bungalow and dancing on the lawn under the banyan tree to the strains of "Fats" Waller, for whose music we shared a mutual respect. I also remember her taking my small daughter, Sarah, out in her pony trap, or "Tum-tum" as they were called.

Margot was a tall, good-looking girl and full of fun. She was a fair tennis player and fond of a party but, unfortunately I only knew her for a few months in Bareilly and I remember her mostly as a charming and dedicated nurse at the hospital.

The war came and we went our different ways, I to the Fourteenth Army and she to Singapore. I only heard vague rumours of her fate and did not see or hear any more of her until we met unexpectedly after the war in the tea tent at the RAMC sports at Aldershot, when the conversation went something like this:

"Hello, Margot, I thought you were dead!"

"Did you, Pat? I am sorry to disappoint you."

And she went on to ask about my wife and family.

At that time, before mepacrine and other modern remedies had become available, there was a lot of malaria in the hot weather which kept the QAs busy. In her first hot-weather season Margot was suddenly sent for to go up to the hill station of Naini Tal to nurse the Civil Surgeon who had been taken seriously ill. The request came at 2 p.m. on a blisteringly hot afternoon and she set off soon after in a staff car with an Indian driver. Motoring up the steep and narrow hill road, hugging precipices with enormous drops into the valleys below, and twisting in a series of fearful hair-pin bends, was a harrowing experience in daylight; but in the dark, with a driver who couldn't talk English and whom she had never seen before, it was an experience she didn't enjoy at all. Cars were not allowed in Naini itself and she had to be carried the last part of the journey in a sedan chair, in which she felt a great deal safer. She stayed with the Civil Surgeon for a month, until he was well enough to travel home to England, after which she returned to Bareilly.

A few months later Margot was sent to nurse a smallpox case in Meerut. She had to be kept completely isolated from the other Sisters in a small wing at the end of the hospital Mess. The woman patient was the wife of one of the British soldiers who had refused to be vaccinated. She wasn't very ill, so Margot didn't have much to do. She was on night duty so she used to get up about 5 p.m., when not many people were about, and visit the historic Meerut cemetery. In consequence, in the three weeks she was on the case, she learnt a great deal about the Indian Mutiny. The cemeteries of Indian military cantonments are a source of historical information and she read with sadness the pathetic inscriptions on the little tombstones of the children, so many of whom died in those far-off days, and the many tombstones dedicated to young British soldiers who lost their lives, not in the heat of war, but from enteric, typhoid, cholera and so on—diseases which had been made much less of a hazard by the time Margot took her lonely walks in Meerut, owing to modern drugs and hygiene. During those three weeks Margot never saw the main Military Hospital—though she saw it later when she was posted to Meerut.

The following summer Margot was one of the Sisters posted for the three months, July to October, to the Ranikhet hospital. This was a wonderful experience and she still maintains that Ranikhet was the most beautiful place she has ever seen; she even tolerated night duty there because she could see the dawn breaking over the Himalayas from the roof of the hospital. It wasn't possible to see Mount Everest itself, but the other great peaks, Nanda Devi and Nanga Parbat would rise up, sharp and brilliant in the clear morning light, until the daytime clouds shrouded them from sight.

Whilst at Ranikhet in 1939 Margot was in charge of the operating theatre, which she enjoyed very much. There was also plenty of tennis, a lovely golf course and, as usual, whenever she had a chance, she rode the local hill "tats"—scruffy little mountain ponies who covered the ground in a curious running motion which bore little resemblance to the normal trot. She was then lent a wonderful pony belonging to the son of the Maharajah of Reiwar. He was attached to a

16

British regiment in Ranikhet and one day, whilst Margot and another Sister were riding past the polo ground where he was schooling his ponies, he asked the Sisters if they would like to help him exercise them. He must certainly have been impressed with their riding to have entrusted them with such valuable ponies. They, of course, gladly agreed and thoroughly enjoyed their riding for the next two months. Unhappily, the young man suddenly contracted cerebral malaria. He was brought into the hospital late one night and died almost immediately. With his death there was no more riding the polo ponies.

Margot had now acquired a little Austin 7 car—1929 vintage. This was a great joy to her and enabled her to enlarge her activities. With the Indian increment she was now earning enough money to do the things she wanted to do. When she first became a QA at Aldershot she was only getting £80 a year; but the Indian rates were higher and she now received something like £100. All the Indian servants in the Mess and hospital were Government paid and the Sisters were allocated one bearer between two of them; but the bearers were attached to the Mess and so when the Sisters went on holiday they didn't have any Indian servant to look after them —which was rather a drawback. Sometimes friends would come up from the plains and stay at the small hotel just opposite the hospital and they would go for picnics down the mountainside. So life was pleasant enough in the cool mountain station, with plenty of work and plenty of leisure.

Margot always kept in first-class physical condition: she didn't drink very much and smoked very little. She loved fresh air and exercise and revelled in the wonderful walks she could take on the hillsides and through the pinewoods. And of course it was her mental and physical fitness which stood her in such good stead when she had to undergo the terrible ordeals which faced her later on.

Margot was in Ranikhet when they heard the declaration of war on the wireless. It plunged the QAs into the depths of depression. They felt so far away and out of things and it was difficult to get news of what was happening. When she left Ranikhet in October Margot was posted to Meerut instead of going back to Bareilly; and she was to remain stationed in Meerut until March 1941. But she went to Ranikhet again from

March to July, as it was also the hill station for Meerut.

She speaks feelingly about Meerut, which she would have enjoyed more if the fact that there was a war on hadn't kept nagging at her mind. She says:

It was a big station with a much larger hospital and Mess than Bareilly and I got to know a lot of people. We had our own tennis courts and there was a very nice club and polo, which I enjoyed watching. And of course Delhi was only fifty miles away. Distances in India didn't mean a thing. Someone would say: "Let's go and dine and dance in Delhi"—and you thought nothing of it, whereas in England, if someone had made the same suggestion about Brighton you would have been surprised. We were young and gay and had lots of friends and we enjoyed ourselves. But we worked very hard too.

As more news continued to come in about the war—Dunkirk, the threat of the invasion of Britain, the bombing of London and the other cities—Margot got more and more restless and eventually made applications to the Commanding Officer through the Principal Matron that she should be allowed to go on active service. But now the fact that she had become such a good theatre sister stood in her way as they were very short of theatre sisters in India. So she had to see other Sisters sent abroad whilst the answers to her own applications were always "No".

Whilst she had been in Ranikhet Margot had a visit from her old friend of the Cambridge hospital days, "Jimmy" James, who was stationed in Lucknow. They planned to take their leave together in Burma and go up the Irrawaddy River. However, not unnaturally, they were not allowed to leave India, so they decided to go to a little place in Orissa on the Bay of Bengal called Puri, where they spent a very pleasant two weeks, sight-seeing, swimming and lazing around in the sun. This was followed by a few days in Calcutta to do some shopping and they then went by train to Delhi where Margot picked up her little 1929 Austin 7 car in which they toured round Delhi and Agra.

Jimmy was then posted to Cawnpore where she got engaged to be married and

Margot went there to stay for a few days to meet her fiancé. Jimmy James was married and became Mrs. D. E. Tattersall and she and Margot didn't meet again until after the war. She too described Margot as a splendid character and sterling friend.

After Margot got back to Meerut she began again, in early 1941, to pull all the strings she could to get herself sent on active service. At last, late in February, she received orders to report at Bombay on 1 March, for posting to an unknown destination, as part of No. 17 Combined General Hospital. She had to put all her things in store and dispose of her beloved dachshund, and her little car was sold to a friend.

Margot was naturally sad at leaving her dog and her friends but was very thrilled to be going on active service at last. She went down to Bombay in a party of eight QAs, four regulars and four reserves. She did not know any of them; but on the train she noticed an unknown Sister, whose name she subsequently discovered was Eileen Gibbs (later Mrs. N. L. Dodd). They all arrived at Bombay on a Sunday morning and were told that they were to stay at the Grand Hotel for several days before embarkation and that they were to share their rooms to save expense. Margot and Eileen Gibbs decided to share a room together. As Eileen was a New Zealander Margot forthwith christened her Kiwi.

They were then told that they would be embarking on the following Thursday, by which time they had spent every penny they had enjoying themselves in Bombay and meeting up with all sorts of people. Everything was very hush-hush and they didn't even know the name of the ship in which they were sailing. However, they forgathered at the quay at the appointed time and were taken out to the ship in launches. Next day they were told that they could go ashore on Saturday morning from 10 to 12, but must be back at the quayside by noon.

The QAs went off for a final fling, meeting up with many friends and finishing up at the Taj Mahal Hotel for a farewell drink before they left. The party was gay and time sped by. Suddenly they realized they hadn't left themselves enough time to get to the quay at the appointed hour. It was the busiest time of the morning and impossible to get a taxi. The poor Matron, Miss Russell, was waiting at the quayside with a midshipman and a launch standing by—and none of her Sisters there. But she couldn't go without them and when they all arrived some twenty minutes late she was so relieved that she couldn't really be cross with them.

2

The Far East

THE ship left Bombay on 8 March 1941. On board was an Indian infantry battalion, the Mysore Infantry of the Indian State Forces, and No. 17 Combined General Hospital. The largest part of the hospital personnel was Indian, there being sixteen Indian Nursing Sisters (IMNS) as compared with the eight QAs of the British Section. The Matron was a QA. The CO was a British officer of the Indian Medical Service and most of the officers, both British and Indian, were IMS, with the exception of three or four British officers who were from the Royal Army Medical Corps (RAMC).

Despite the fact that she had served two and a half years in India this was Margot's first experience of working with Indian doctors and nurses. All the latter could speak English and they got on with one another very well—though at first the QAs tended, rather naturally, to keep together.

In the convoy there were two or three transports and several escorting vessels. Naturally everyone wanted to know where they were going. Margot had somehow taken it for granted that they would be going west, where the war was, but when they set sail in the afternoon and saw the sun setting she realized that her hopes were to be dashed. And when the Captain opened his sealed orders at midnight it was discovered that their destination was Singapore. If Margot, and the other QAs aboard, had known more about the world situation they would have realized that they were going towards a future battleground—and one which was to become one of the most critical and controversial of them all. But all she could feel at the time was bitterness and frustration that, after all her efforts, she was going even farther away from active service than she had been in India. To the QAs Singapore seemed like the back of beyond.

However, it was no good moaning about it. It was characteristic of Margot that she accepted every turn of fate which she couldn't alter and made the best of it. They had ten days of the voyage before them and they played deck games, got to know one another, and looked forward to seeing a new country and a new people.

Their arrival in Singapore was an experience in itself. There it lay, the fabulous island fortress, serene, impregnable, green and colourful—a paradise upon earth. But they didn't get much opportunity of seeing it then as they were informed that they were to entrain that same night for Kuala Lumpur and thence go on to Tanjong Malim. However, before leaving Singapore, the QAs were whisked off to dine and dance at the famous Raffles Hotel. They were all in uniform, wearing their white dresses, and they thought that everything was wonderful.

Kuala Lumpur was about a third of the way up the Malayan peninsula. They left Singapore by train at about 10 p.m. and arrived at Kuala Lumpur at 6 a.m. the following morning. There they were met by the ADMS, who had his headquarters at Kuala Lumpur, and had breakfast at the station hotel. They then took train for Tanjong Malim, which was a very small place with one street and a few shops, far away from anywhere and about sixty or seventy miles further north. There they took over the hospital—a big Malay teaching college. They also took over the bungalows that the teachers had lived in. The Nursing Sisters had one bungalow for their Mess and three or four more for their sleeping-quarters. There was a rest-house in the village where they were able to get meals of a sort until they got organized. Margot and Kiwi shared a big room in one of the bungalows; and there they unpacked their camp kit, put up their camp beds on the verandah and made the one room into a sitting-room.

The climate was hot and humid and it always seemed to rain at four or five in the afternoon, just as they were about to play tennis. But it very soon stopped and the courts dried out quickly. Tropical thunderstorms often blew up, which some people, including Kiwi, found very frightening; but they didn't worry Margot. Tropical storms can of course be very alarming, when the lightning zips past one's ears with the sound of tearing calico and the thunder comes cracking down almost simultaneously. It was typical perhaps of Margot's calm nature that she should disregard nature's fireworks.

The nearest troops were at Kuala Lumpur, and, as none of their hospital equipment arrived for another three weeks and they had no patients, they were rather at a loose end and wondered why a large combined hospital should have been put in such an isolated place in this beautiful country of apparent peace and plenty. But they settled down to enjoy life as best they could until some real work materialized.

The island of Singapore is about the same size as the Isle of Wight and is separated from the Malayan mainland by the Straits of Johore which in many places are less than one mile in width. The only crossing over the Straits was the Johore causeway, a little over one thousand yards in length, which carried two railway lines, the road and the large water mains. Running up the middle of the Malayan peninsula is a range of mountains, rising to some seven thousand feet, which forms a backbone to the peninsula, with subsidiary ranges running parallel to it. On the east and west of these ranges are the coastlines, the eastern one with sandy beaches and palm trees, the western one much more developed and thickly populated, and largely consisting of mangrove swamps. The greater part of Malaya is jungle, the soil of which is very fertile, due to the combined effects of a tropical sun and torrential rain. In this soil grows a profusion of trees and flowers of every possible description, shape and colour—bamboo trees, creepers of every range, orchids, banana trees and every other sort of fruit tree.

To the newcomer the Malayan jungle is beautiful; but after a while the very profusion and the pungent aroma become nauseating. On the western side the jungle is laced by rivers, streams and creeks, which the Malays use a great deal for inland travel. The jungle, which appears almost impenetrable to the uninitiated, contains many jungle paths and tracks. In wartime, the jungle is a terrifying place to the untrained soldier; but for the man trained and equipped to fight in it—as the Japanese were in 1942 and General Slim's 14th Army was later on—it can be used to advantage.

In the extreme north of Malaya, where much rice is grown, the country is, in places, more open than it is in the south. There are some comparatively open areas in the tin-mining country in the States of Perak and Selangor. The main line of communication was the railway, which ran north from Singapore, up the west coast, to Thailand; and there was a good trunk road all the way up the west coast. On the east coast the communications were bad. All the main operations of the war took place on the west coast.

The major industry in Malaya was of course rubber, and the rubber plantations stretched for many miles over the peninsula—particularly on the west coast. All the rubber estates were well equipped with excellent motor roads: and it was the motor cars, and the roads to carry them, which had led to the great development of the rubber industry in Malaya. When it came to military operations the rubber plantations gave useful cover—particularly to the British troops when the Japanese gained complete command of the air. Before the expansion of the rubber industry coffee had been the main product of the country; but artificial rubber was being produced in such great quantities in the United States that it is probable that the natural rubber in Malaya would soon have become a drug on the market. The other great source of Malaya's wealth was tin and the country contained some of the greatest tin mines in the world.

The Malayan jungle contains every sort of wild animal, including tigers and crocodiles. And yet it was very seldom that the troops saw a wild animal. The climate was hot and humid all the year round and very enervating for the European. As in India and Burma also, troops started the war wearing topis (pith helmets) and then gradually discarded them, without ill effect, for some sort of Australian or Gurkha broad-brimmed hat.

The population of Malaya was very mixed. There were about two million Malays and roughly the same number of Chinese. But the Chinese had much more influence on the trade of the country and provided the bulk of the labour in the rubber and tin industries. There were nearly thirty thousand Europeans and over seven hundred thousand Indians. There were also nearly eight thousand Japanese and there is no doubt that a large number of these were trained and used by the Japanese Intelligence Services. The British in Malaya were firstly, the officials of the Civil Service, the engineers, forest officers, doctors, surveyors and police officers; and secondly, the traders, who were mostly connected with the rubber and tin industries. None of them of course looked on Malaya as their home.

Some people really imagined that, in 1941, the defence of Singapore still depended on the Royal Navy and the powerful coastal defence guns on Singapore Island which, they maintained, were pointing the wrong way—that is, out to sea. So of course they were. However, it had been realized years before that the Japanese would not be so foolish as to attack Singapore Island from the sea but would undoubtedly do so from a northern invasion of the mainland of Malaya. True, the vast Naval Base on the north-east of Singapore Island, with its great anchorage and docks, which had taken so many years to build at a cost of so many millions of pounds, still remained; and, until the operations started, gave great confidence to all the inhabitants that Singapore was still the impregnable fortress it had always been supposed to be. But, only a few years before the Second World War started, it was decided that the defence of Malaya would be based on an Air Force plan, which was designed to smash a Japanese invasion as far as possible from the shores of Malaya. To do this effectively a number of widely dispersed aerodromes were hastily constructed—several of them in the eastern portion of the peninsula. And the land forces had to be dispersed to protect them. Obviously, if the aircraft provided were not of the highest quality and adequate in numbers, the plan fell to pieces at the outset—which was exactly what happened. The dispositions the Army were required to take up were faulty because they entailed the wide dispersion of troops. And they were doubly faulty when the large air forces which had been promised did not materialize and the aerodromes fell like ripe plums into the hands of the Japanese.

When the plan was made it was estimated that a minimum of 336 first-line aircraft would be required to implement it. In September 1940, after the fall of France, Japanese troops occupied the northern part of French Indo-China, which gave them a base much nearer to Malaya than they had ever had before. At the same time Japan signed a Tripartite Pact with Germany and Italy and thus became definitely committed to the Axis connection. As a result of this dangerous development a joint tactical appreciation, which was prepared in

Malaya, estimated that 566 first-line aircraft would now be required. The Chiefs of Staff in London accepted this as an ideal but found it quite beyond the limit of their resources and considered that 336 first-line aircraft would give a fair degree of security. But when the operations started General Percival had only 141 operationally serviceable aircraft—and these included 48 antiquated Brewster Buffalo fighters, which did not compare with the Japanese Navy Zero fighter. Hence, of course, the complete air superiority over the whole theatre of operations—both land and sea—which the Japanese obtained in the first forty-eight hours of the operations—and the sinking of the great battleships, the *Prince of Wales* and the *Repulse*, which followed almost automatically.

It is interesting to compare the air situation at the time of the Japanese invasion of Malaya in 1941 with that which faced the Allied powers in the invasion of Fortress Europe in June 1944. The latter sought to impose on the defending Germans exactly the same supreme air superiority as the Japanese imposed on the British in Malaya —without which they considered that the amphibious invasion of Fortress Europe would be impossible. And so thoroughly did the Allies achieve this air superiority in 1944 that on D Day—upon which the success of the whole invasion depended—scarcely a single German aircraft appeared over the Channel or Normandy. So far as the air situation was concerned the Allied invading armies had the key advantage—without which they could not have set forth at all— of virtual immunity from air attack during embarkation, transit and disembarkation. And moreover, looking further back into Fortress Europe, the defending German armies were completely paralysed by the destruction of their rail and road communications.

In December 1941 the military resources of the British Commonwealth—sea, air and land—were stretched to the limit in the war against Germany. The Hurricanes and Spitfires were needed in the west; the tanks for which General Percival repeatedly asked (and all the main thrusts of the Japanese in Malaya were strongly supported by tanks) were required elsewhere; no more troops were available from India—and yet, when it was too late and the war in Malaya was virtually lost, thousands of troops were rushed to Singapore. The truth is, of course, that complacency about the impregnability of the Singapore base was much more apparent in London than in the Malayan Command—where there was no complacency at all.

When General Percival took over the Malayan Command in May 1941 his land forces were disposed mainly to oppose the most probable Japanese line of attack from the extreme north of the Peninsula down the west coast, with detached formations watching the possible landing places on the east coast and defending the aerodromes.

But these were all problems for the higher command to worry about. For the ordinary people life went on as usual; and for Margot Turner and her fellow nurses at Tanjong Malim the spring of 1941 was, to start with, distinctly tedious. At last, however, all their equipment arrived and they were able to get the hospital organized. It was divided into two wings, one British and one Indian—the latter being much the larger. To start with they functioned separately but in the end the two wings, and all the Nursing Sisters, were mixed up together.

Margot was in charge of the operating theatre, which was the job she liked most. But they had time on their hands and had to make their own interests and amusements. They went for walks, travelled on the ration lorry to see the sights and shop in Kuala Lumpur, played poker in the evenings and wondered why they had ever been sent to this out-of-the-way spot. Margot wrote to her mother that they were supposed to be on active service but she had never been so inactive in her life.

In June another hospital arrived from India—the 20th Combined General Hospital—which was posted to Taiping in Perak, much further north. This hospital never did get all its equipment and had to send its X-Ray patients down to the 17th.

By now the QAs were fairly busy and the equipment was all installed; they also started to get quite a number of patients from different parts of the country. But they were a very small community in Tanjong Malim. Their nearest neighbours were the planters—the closest being five miles away. There was a little planters' club in the village, about two hundred yards from the hospital, which had fallen into disuse. But when the hospital arrived the planters decided to get it going again and they used to have gramophone dances there about once a fortnight, which made a pleasant break. The planters were very hospitable and used to ask the Sisters to their homes for lunch or dinner—they were probably pleased to see some new faces.

News of the war filtered in over the radio, but it was concerned solely with the war in North Africa. It wasn't until about August or September that people began to ask themselves about the Japanese and to wonder what might happen in Malaya. But in Malaya everything was more or less normal. There were many Australian units in the country at that time. They had their own hospitals and the doctors and sisters were very friendly and used to come to Tanjong Malim to visit and bring in supplies. Margot was to see a lot more of their Nursing Sisters in the dark days to come.

The Australian Red Cross had taken a small bungalow in a place called Frazers Hill, a little hill station some fifty miles away, with a golf course and a few bungalows, and they offered a fortnight's free holiday to the 17th CGH Sisters, two people to go at a time. So Margot and Kiwi put in to go and were allotted the first trip in early November. They had a wonderful time playing golf and walking in the woods and their friends came up to visit them at weekends. They were the first and last to go from the hospital to Frazers Hill for this free holiday.

Soon rumours of war came thick and fast and troop movements were more in evidence, particularly when they went to Kuala Lumpur where General Sir Lewis Heath, the commander of the 3rd Indian Corps, had his headquarters. The one-armed general, generally known to the troops as "Piggy", was a popular and friendly commander. Although no one had any real anxiety there was a general feeling of suspense in the air—like the atmosphere just before a thunderstorm.

The weekend immediately before the war started Margot was asked by one of the medical officers in the hospital to dine with him in Kuala Lumpur and the CO, Colonel Hurford, offered to give them a lift in his car. They went in about 4 p.m., did some shopping, had a swim, and then went to a hotel where they had dinner and danced.

They had planned to meet Colonel Hurford at midnight at the Club, which was commonly known as "The Spotted Dog". At the hotel Margot noticed that a number of the people dancing were in uniform, though she and her escort were in plain clothes. After a time the Military Police arrived and ordered all military personnel to report back to their units immediately. Margot and her friend couldn't go back to Tanjong Malim until the Colonel arrived; but they went to the Club to await him. They had barely started to dance when the Military Police again arrived and gave the same order—so they thought it would be less conspicuous if they just sat quietly and waited for the Colonel. He arrived soon after midnight; he had been with a party to the cinema and knew nothing about the hoo-ha.

On the way back to Tanjong Malim they were stopped by a road block and had their names and particulars checked. It seemed obvious that something was about to happen. And from that date on they had to wear uniform all the time. The rumours now really did begin to fly. Margot had a little radio which began to buzz with excitement. And, when the bearer brought her early-morning tea on Monday 8 December she heard on the radio that Singapore had been bombed at 4 a.m. that morning. So that was it. She was in the war at last.

3

The Fall of Singapore

THE Sisters all gathered for breakfast in a rather sombre atmosphere, wondering what would happen next. But they could only get a vague idea of what was occurring from the rather cryptic news bulletins and the official statements put out by the Malayan Broadcasting Corporation —and from such bits of gossip as they could gather from people passing through. The Governor and the Malayan Command quite naturally wanted to keep the morale of the troops and the civilian population as high as possible—and this was no easy matter so far as the administrative services and the civilians were concerned when, very soon, the only aircraft seen or heard were Japanese. In fact, by 11 December, only three days after the first air raid on Singapore, practically all the British aerodromes in Northern Malaya had become untenable and, in view of the enemy's great fighter superiority, British bombers could only operate by night. There is nothing so depressing for a civilian population—and indeed for the military too—to have to face than complete enemy air superiority, which makes all movement on the roads and railways dangerous and existence generally very uncomfortable. Good troops will take a lot of hammering if they know the enemy is being hammered too, but to be bombed and machine-gunned continually by Japanese planes circling round in the air with no opposition whatever became very dispiriting indeed after a time. And the Malays, the Chinese and the Indians living in Malaya and Singapore, didn't really feel—like the people of London for instance—that this was their war and that they were right in it; in fact, those who could conveniently do so soon took steps to get right out of it. And that made things very difficult for administrative units—such as No. 17 Combined General Hospital for instance—which perforce had to depend to a considerable extent on local servants and labour.

But the really shattering blow to British prestige and morale, which reverberated from Malaya throughout the entire British

Commonwealth—and sounded as hideous in Canberra, London and Delhi as it did in Singapore and Tanjong Malim—was the disaster at sea which took place off Kuantan on the east coast on 10 December.

On 2 December two great British battle-ships, the *Prince of Wales* and the *Repulse*, had arrived in Singapore. This was a gesture inspired by Winston Churchill, with the object of either deterring the Japanese from invading Malaya or causing them grievous damage whilst so doing. It could not have achieved the first part of the objective be-cause it was much too late. The Japanese invasion mechanism was already in opera-tion. But it could well have achieved the second part if only—*if only*—the aircraft promised to General Percival by the Chiefs of Staff in London had arrived and the British, instead of the Japanese, had control-led the sea, land and air around Malaya. As each month of 1941 went by the Air Officer Commanding, Air Vice-Marshal Pulford, never ceased to represent to higher authority the grave weakness of the air situation in Malaya. It has been argued that the naval disaster would never have happened if an aircraft carrier had accompanied the two battleships. That might have postponed it; but, in view of the great superiority of the Japanese land-based aircraft, the result would have been the same in the end. It was the initial air battles over Malaya that the British should have won—but which they so devastatingly lost, owing to circumstances completely beyond their own control.

Nevertheless, what a heart-warming affair it was when the two great battleships arrived in Singapore, escorted by four destroyers. There was no secret about their arrival; the British wanted the Japanese and the people of Malaya to know what had dropped in just at this critical moment—and for the Japanese to be suitably deterred from starting anything. Margot's little wireless set almost burst with pride and joy. But no one was told when the battleships quietly left Singapore on Monday 8 December to operate against the reported threat of Japanese landings on the east coast.

At 11.15 a.m. on 10 December Japanese torpedo-bombers attacked the two capital ships and, by 1.20 p.m., both ships had been sunk. The news of this disaster spread rapidly through Malaya and, at 8.30 p.m., it was broadcast over the Singapore radio.

Needless to say, the Japanese made the very most of it.

It was on this same day, 10 December, that the 17th Combined General Hospital received its first convoy of battle casualties, coming down the line from the northern battle. And on this day Margot saw her first air raid—on Kuala Lumpur. From then on the news was uniformly bad. Few newspapers were received in the hospital but the radio coverage was quite good, though it indicated a rapidly deteriorating situation for the British in Northern Malaya.

In the latter part of December the Far East War Council gave earnest consideration to the evacuation of women and children and they eventually decided that all the *bouches inutiles*—people who were doing no war work—should be sent away.

The Japanese, who had been training for this type of operation for a long time, had delivered their assaults with tremendous impetus, using their favourite pincer movement to envelop the flanks as soon as they were held up in the centre: and as they were rice eaters they could live off the country and were not tied to their communications as were the British.

The sounds of battle were now coming nearer to Tanjong Malim; more and more battle casualties were coming in; and then, on Christmas Eve, orders were received for the hospital to move back. An ambulance train arrived and took off all the patients. The train had its own staff of doctors and nurses and those of No. 17 Combined General Hospital were left behind to come on later in another train. But a day or two later the Japanese bombed and completely destroyed Tanjong Malim station, thus preventing any more trains coming through. None of the bombs actually hit the hospital but the noise was shattering—and when the raid was over the hospital servants, Chinese and Indian, had decided that discretion was the better part of valour and disappeared into the jungle.

That night the staff of No. 17 were told that an ambulance train was coming up the line and that they were to take what they could carry and walk down the line to meet it. The fighting units, who are self-sufficient when placed on a war footing, don't realize how much an administrative unit in the East depends on its native labour. When the cooks, the bearers, the water-carriers and so on, disappear from a hospital, the doctors and the nurses become hungry beasts of burden until they can find another base.

Eventually, after a long walk, they found the train and went on board. They had a very hazardous journey, with continuous stops to try to dodge the bombing, until they reached Seremban, about twenty-five miles south of Kuala Lumpur, where they were ordered to detrain. There they ran into some quite heavy bombing and took refuge in a convenient drain. Two days were spent in the rest-house at Seremban and they then boarded another ambulance train. The engine driver and all the civilian staff had fled but a couple of British soldiers managed to get the train moving. The Doctors and Sisters had brought their Christmas dinner with them—which had been cooked but never eaten—and the soldiers on the train heated it up for them. Everyone agreed it was the most wonderful Christmas dinner they had ever had—turkey, plum pudding, mince pies, the lot, eaten several days after Christmas and washed down with neat whisky.

When they arrived in Singapore they were sent to the Alexandra Hospital, about five miles west of Singapore City. The air seemed full of Japanese aircraft, some dropping bombs, others machine-gunning communications and yet others dropping thousands of propaganda leaflets. There were signs of many more troops arriving in Singapore; but the news from the front didn't sound good at all. It was a case not so much of "too little and too late", but of the wrong things very, very much too late.

The Alexandra Hospital was chock-full of casualties and new buildings had to be taken over. After a few days four QAs, the Matron, Miss Russell, Eileen "Kiwi" Gibbs, Margot Turner and Brenda Wells—who was later killed—were sent to Changi in the extreme north-east corner of the Island, to organize the re-opening of No. 17 Combined General Hospital. They took over the Barracks and were given the Station Officers' Mess, which was on a hill overlooking the Johore Straits. It was a beautiful Mess and they were very busy but very happy during the short time they were there. Almost as soon as they had arrived in the Mess there was an air raid warning and they had to dive into a slit trench. The roof-spotter shrieked to them to get out at once. And how right he was! The trench was alive with leeches and red ants. They never got into another one.

After a few days' comparative peace the rest of the unit started to arrive. They had received reinforcements of nursing staff from India—most of them British. The hospital then became a very busy place and Margot found herself back in her old job in charge of the operating theatre.

A steady stream of battle casualties—both British and Indian—were now coming to the hospital, a large number of whom were air bombing cases. When the hospital had its first serious air raid Kiwi remembers that Margot kept marvellously cool; and thereafter she was always the first to be with the patients and orderlies in any emergency. Margot's Indian surgeon didn't like operating during a raid, which was understandable —few surgeons would—but as they began to get a number of raids every day it wasn't possible to avoid and eventually they were operating continuously all day and far into the night.

Margot says:

We were working very hard, making up for all the work we hadn't done during the few months before the war started. Now we really felt we were doing something at last and taking our proper place. We no longer thought we were in a backwater; in fact we didn't have much time to think at all. There was no question of off duty. You might get off for an hour or two in the evening, but then you had to go back again.

For a time they were lucky in that, although there were a number of near misses, no bombs actually fell on the hospital. Then the officers' ward received a direct hit. The place was a shambles. As many casualties as possible were extricated; and the Sisters were on continuous duty, with the operating theatre working non-stop.

On the night of 30/31 January the final withdrawal of the British forces across the Causeway, separating the Malayan peninsula from Singapore Island, took place.

General Percival made the following public announcement:

The battle of Malaya has come to an end and the battle of Singapore has started. For nearly two months our troops have fought an enemy on the mainland who has held the advantage of great air superiority and considerable freedom of movement by sea.

Our task has been both to impose losses on the enemy and to gain time to enable the forces of the Allies to be concentrated for this struggle in the Far East. Today we stand beleaguered in our island fortress. Our task is to hold this fortress until help can come—as assuredly it will come. This we are determined to do. In carrying out this task we want the help of every man and woman in the fortress. There is work for all to do. Any enemy who sets foot in the fortress must be dealt with immediately. The enemy within our gates must be ruthlessly weeded out. There must be no more loose talk and rumour-mongering. Our duty is clear. With firm resolve and fixed determination we shall win through.

But to all those on the Island the blowing of the Causeway was a very shattering and depressing sound.

The Changi hospital—and particularly the Mess—was now in a very exposed position, facing on to the Johore Straits, the north side of which was occupied by the Japanese, and they could shell as well as bomb the north-east area of Singapore Island. All the servants had departed and the menial tasks, as well as the nursing, had to be done by the Sisters. In spite of the large Red Crosses on all the buildings, the Japs bombed, shelled and machine-gunned quite indiscriminately. It was terrible to see the helpless patients and to hear their screams when the bombs came nearer. The noise was terrific and the hospital positively rocked at times.

On 6 February orders were received that the patients were to be moved from Changi into Singapore and the staff were ordered to vacate the Mess and move into the hospital.

Margot and Kiwi were the last Sisters to leave and were caught in a very unpleasant bit of shelling from across the Straits, which compelled them to seek shelter under the billiard table. However, early on the next day, they were all evacuated to the Alexandra Hospital and were then immediately split up into two parties, the British staff being sent to reinforce another new British hospital, while the Indian staff went to a big Indian hospital at Tyersall Park, which was situated in a large hutted camp north-west of Singapore. On 11 February this latter hospital was badly bombed with terrible results. The wooden huts burnt fiercely and very few of the large number of staff and patients survived.

The British forces, who had for two months fought such a stubborn rearguard action throughout the length and breadth of Malaya, were desperately tired, considerably disorganized and had suffered heavy casualties; and the new formations, which had arrived from India at the last moment, were completely untrained for jungle warfare—and in any case were too late to influence the battle. The Japanese gave them no respite. On the night of 8/9 February an intense artillery bombardment could be heard from the north of the Island. The crash of shells and the chattering of machine-guns never stopped. Oil tanks were ablaze at many points and a pall of smoke and murk spread over the Island. This was accompanied by some air bombing further south.

On the morning of the 9th Singapore radio broadcast a short announcement that the Japanese had landed on the north-west of the Island and would be counter-attacked and driven off. But by the 10th it was painfully obvious that the Japanese were enlarging their bridgehead and pushing relentlessly inland.

The rumble of artillery fire was continuous, the pall of smoke still hung overhead. British and Australian troops were taking up new positions; motor transport rushed about on the roads; there were several raids on the docks; and the native population, numbed by the horror of it all, took shelter wherever they could. The Japanese had now reached Bukit Timah, only five miles from Singapore City.

"It must be admitted," wrote General Percival, when he returned from captivity, "that the Japanese feat in mounting this attack in the space of about a week was a fine military performance. The fighting of their troops was also of a very high order. The landing operations were conducted with the greatest determination in spite of what must have been very heavy losses."

There was still one squadron of RAF fighter aircraft operating most gallantly against hopeless odds from Kallang aerodrome on the east side of Singapore City. But the aerodrome was now so full of bomb craters that it was hardly usable. On 10 February the last British aircraft left Singapore.

On the night of 8/9 February the new hospital, to which Margot Turner and the British Section of No. 17 Combined General Hospital had been posted only the day before, was very badly bombed and the place nearly flattened. Next morning everybody was evacuated to the Alexandra Hospital which, miraculously, had not been hit at all. There was by then a great congestion in the hospital, both of patients and of nurses; but there were no Mess servants and Margot was one of the Sisters detailed to do some of the cooking and cleaning.

The best part of four thousand *bouches inutiles* had been evacuated from Singapore on 30 January; but there were still a few thousand more women and children on the Island and, in addition, certain units of British and Australian nurses and a number of key naval and military personnel. General Percival ordered that as many civilians as possible were now to be got away at once. On Tuesday 10 February the Principal Matron,

Miss Jones, held a meeting of all the Sisters and explained that there was a boat leaving the next day which was to take some of the staff. All the (British) VADs were to go, half of the QAs and half of the IMNS Nurses. With regard to the two latter categories Matron asked for volunteers to go—but no one responded.

It was a terrible decision for the Matron to make—and how she made it no one quite knew. But the outcome was that Kiwi was told to go and Margot to stay. It was a harrowing moment for those two great friends, neither of whom really thought they would ever meet again.

Kiwi records her lasting impression of Margot when she left Singapore as, ". . . always the most popular person in the hospital—everyone spoke well of her, patients and staff alike. She was quite unflappable."

In this first contingent of nurses to leave Singapore on 11 February was Mrs. Evelyn Cowans of the 1st Malayan General Hospital. She describes her departure and voyage thus:*

*From the Nursing Service Records.

Singapore was a pathetic sight; no civilians to be seen, just isolated groups of exhausted soldiers and machine-gun posts. Buildings and cars in flames; many planes overhead, but all of them Japanese. The difficulty was to find our ship, the *Empire Star*. The docks were a mass of flame and smoke and no one knew the way. Finally we found the ship; she had twenty-four cabins and took on board two and a half thousand passengers, mostly troops and RAF personnel. There were also fifty Australian and eighty British nurses and a few civilians and children.

At 4 p.m. we moved out of the harbour to wait for the convoy. We fondly hoped that our troubles were over—how wrong we were! Next morning we were bombed by a large number of Japanese planes and the ship suffered seven direct hits which caused many casualties. But the damage was quickly dealt with by the crew, assisted by volunteers from the military passengers. It was a terrifying experience. Several times the ship pitched over as though she were going to capsize but managed to right herself. We were kept busy attending to the wounded. We organized three sick rooms and laid the patients out on mattresses on the floor. All the Nursing Sisters were down below in the hold, where the huge cargoes of frozen meat were usually carried.

However, the *Empire Star* was one of the lucky ships which reached Batavia safely; and from there her passengers were shipped to India. By June 1942 Mrs. Cowans was back in England, where she made a valuable report to the Matron-in-Chief.

Margot, and her fellow nurses who were left, while not perhaps exactly happy, were resigned to the fact that they had refused the offer of evacuation and would now see the thing through with their patients. What might have happened to them if they had stayed is anybody's guess. And many of those who were ordered to go in the first batch met their death on the voyage at the hands of the Japanese bombers.

The very next day Margot had one of her narrowest escapes from death when the Mess got a direct hit while she was sheltering under the stairs. They were now being shelled as well as bombed by the swiftly advancing Japanese troops. Margot found the shelling much more terrifying than the bombing.

There were still a number of small ships and sea-going craft lying in Singapore harbour, including some naval patrol vessels. It was no longer safe to keep these at Singapore and so Rear-Admiral Spooner decided to sail them all to Java that night and to go with them himself. There were about fifty of these little ships, with accommodation for about three thousand people in addition to the crews. It was the last opportunity that could be foreseen for any organized parties to leave Singapore and vacancies were allotted to the Services and to the Civil Government, the Army being allotted eighteen hundred vacancies. But General Percival ordered that, in view of the report which he had just received on the barbaric treatment suffered by British nurses in Hong Kong, the Nursing Sisters should have the first claim on these vacancies and should be compulsorily evacuated.

What was this report about? Quite briefly this: the worst of the Japanese barbarities in Hong Kong occurred on Christmas morning 1941, just after the surrender, at St. Stephen's College Emergency Hospital where there lay a number of British and Canadian wounded. All the cots were occupied and many of the men were lying on the floor. A Red Cross flag was over the doorway.

When the Japanese burst into the hospital the two senior doctors went to meet them, pointing to the Red Cross and to the wounded men. Both doctors were ruthlessly bayoneted; the Japanese stormed into the hospital and, despite the efforts of the nurses to stop them, ripped the bandages off the wounded and bayoneted a large number of them in their beds. Then they took the nurses, three of whom they afterwards killed, and repeatedly raped them over a period of twenty-four hours. Captain Barnett, a chaplain with the Royal Rifles of Canada, was attached to St. Stephen's Hospital and, on Christmas morning, was preparing to administer Holy Communion when the Japanese burst in. He saw sights that day which made it necessary for him to go to Tokyo in December 1946 to give evidence at the war criminal trials. Some horrors he witnessed personally; of others he had the all too convincing evidence of agonized cries just off stage and mutilated bodies seen shortly afterwards. The bodies of three nurses were found and a special Service held for them and the two doctors. After dark that evening it was possible to evacuate those nurses who had escaped the savagery of the Japanese to Stanley Fort, where it was felt they might be safer.*

This was by no means the only instance of Nursing Sisters being raped in those dark days of 1941 in Hong Kong. Lieut.-Colonel M. Kathleen Thomson writes from Auckland, New Zealand, as follow:

During the actual fighting in Hong Kong in 1941 I was Matron of St. Albert's Military Hospital and I was seriously wounded and one of my Sisters, Brenda Morgan, was killed when the hospital was shelled. I was evacuated to the Queen Mary (Civilian) Hospital and was there for several weeks. Whilst there I heard that one of the Civilian Auxiliary Hospitals at the Jockey Club had been captured and some of the nurses raped by the Japanese. After the capture of St. Stephen's Military Hospital several VADs were raped and then shot.

*From *In This Sign Conquer by Sir John Smyth.*

The behaviour of the Japanese Military forces in Hong Kong was probably the most barbarous that the British had ever experienced at the hands of a so-called "civilized" enemy.

General Percival, having received these reports, was therefore probably entirely justified in taking the decision to evacuate all the Nursing Sisters from Singapore; and Margot Turner may well have owed her life to it. Years after he did regret his decision when he heard of the number of Sisters who had perished at sea; but that was something he could not foretell at the time. It was just as well he didn't know, or his three years' captivity would have been even more bitter than it was.

Having made this decision General Percival went to Government House to discuss the situation with the Governor, Sir Shenton Thomas. Percival knew quite well that the remaining hours of freedom for himself and his Army were now strictly numbered. All his subordinate commanders knew it—and the men knew it too. The unit and brigade commanders were just not able to mount any effective counter-attacks against the swiftly advancing Japanese.

And, above all, lay the menace in the sky, which had been with him all along—the complete air superiority of the Japanese. In this last phase it was this over-riding factor which predominated. Already the Japanese bombing and shelling had severely damaged the water mains and the Municipal Water Engineer had estimated that the water supply—on which the whole city of Singapore depended—might only last another twenty-four hours. And the food and ammunition situation was equally grave. But it was the imminent danger of a total breakdown in the water supply, and the carnage which might result if the Japanese forces fought on right into Singapore City, which decided General Percival to capitulate two days later to the Japanese Commander-in-Chief, General Yamashita. Little did Percival think that, three years later, he would be present to witness General Yamashita's own capitulation.

But now, on this 13th day of February, when he visited Government House, he found that the Governor and Lady Thomas had moved to the Singapore Club as Government House had received a direct hit from a shell which had penetrated into one of the shelters under the house and killed a dozen men.

Percival writes of this visit: "As I looked over the town from the grounds of Government House I could hear shooting everywhere and as I drove back to Fort Canning some shots were fired close to my car." Later that evening he went to say goodbye to Pulford, the Air Officer Commanding, whom he had ordered to leave, together with Rear-Admiral Spooner. Pulford's last words to Percival were: "I suppose you and I will be held responsible for this, but God knows we did our best with the little we were given."

The adventures and sad end of Spooner and Pulford bear some relation to what Margot Turner was about to undergo in the same waters. They left Singapore for Java in a fast patrol boat, but north of the Banka Straits they were chased by a Japanese destroyer and had to run their craft aground on a deserted island. The Japanese dismantled the patrol boat's engines and left them there. Efforts to get the news to Java, and efforts made by GHQ in Java to find them, failed. There was little food on the island and one by one the party sickened and died. After three months the survivors of the party, some twenty odd, out of an original muster of over forty, were found and taken off by the Japanese. But amongst those who died on the island were the two senior officers, Rear-Admiral Spooner and Air Vice-Marshal Pulford.

Percival writes of the evacuation which was to take place on the evening of 13 February:

There was much confusion as a result of enemy bombing and some of those detailed to leave never got on board. There were also some "gate-crashers" as I suppose is to be expected in such circumstances. On the 14th the flotilla encountered the Japanese naval and air forces which were then assembling for the attack on Palembang in southern Sumatra the following day. Many ships were sunk and some were run aground. Few reached their destination. The loss of life was appalling—and that among some of the best who had stood by Singapore to the last. It took months and years to trace the missing. Some of them were never traced. It was a great tragedy.

It is of course easy to be wise after the event; but if the decision to evacuate had been made a week earlier, instead of when the wolf was actually at the door, it would have been a great deal easier. On the other hand this would have been bad for morale and that was probably why Percival didn't do it.

It was at mid-day on the 13th that the Matron assembled the QAs and told them that they were to go, because of the atrocities in Hong Kong, and that they were all to rendezvous at the Singapore Cricket Club at 4 p.m. They felt very sad at leaving all their patients and decided it would be best not to tell them but just to slip quietly away, having said goodbye to the doctors. Margot felt badly about leaving the doctors, among whom she had many friends. Her particular friends were a Major Bennett, who died, Major Duncan Black of the RAMC, and Austin Best of the IMS, none of whom she ever saw again.

The party, which included other Nursing Sisters apart from the QAIMNS, collected at the cricket ground and consisted of about fifty in all. It included most of the senior members of the Service, amongst them Miss Jones, Principal Matron from Alexandra

Hospital, Miss West, Matron of No. 1 Malayan General, Miss Spedding, Matron from 20th CGH, and Miss Russell, Matron from 17 CGH, together with Miss Coward, Home Sister at Alexandra.

In Margot's own words:

We walked from the cricket ground down to the quay. I had a little Hong Kong basket with a change of clothes. That was all I could take. As a matter of fact it was all I had—as all my possessions were destroyed when the Mess was bombed. The evacuation was a complete and utter shambles; there were continuous air raids on the docks and several people were killed on the quayside. There were many touching scenes of husbands being parted from their weeping wives. Some people came down in cars and pushed them into the water or abandoned them on the quayside. I felt very depressed. It was difficult to recognize this as the lovely Singapore where I had arrived less than a year ago.

The Sisters were taken out in a launch to a little ship called the *Kuala*, with shrapnel bursting around them. It was already full of women and children and more and more people flocked aboard. The total amounted to about four hundred women and children evacuees, three hundred PWD officers and the Nursing Sisters. The QAs, with their Matron, kept together. They decided to sit down on the deck and not to worry. In fact there were four Matrons on board and all of them were killed on that ship. The QAs were asked to change their white dresses for something less conspicuous and Margot managed to borrow a grey dress.

The *Kuala* sailed, together with another ship, the *Tien Kwang*, at 7 p.m. On shore there seemed to be fires everywhere and along the waterfront the burning godowns glowed redly in the gathering darkness. The din of battle was deafening, with the British guns replying to the Japanese shelling with everything they had left. Singapore was not the only burning island that night. Hundreds of oil and petrol tanks closely clustered on the islets of Bukum, Sabarok and Sambo had been set on fire by our own forces the previous night and were now lighting up the harbour and sea for miles around, creating a weird, murky twilight. From these islands of fire, thick, black, oily smoke arose in columns to a great height and then formed huge mushrooms which united to spread a glare-tinged pall over the scene.

4

The Will to Live

MARGOT TURNER recalls:

The *Kuala* made slow progress through the night. The QAs huddled together and dozed fitfully. The next morning, at first light, the ship anchored off a little island called Pompong. This was one of a large number of small islands scattered about those seas. The captain said he was going to stay there during the day and sail again at night. A number of the men on board went ashore to collect branches and leaves to camouflage the ship. I had no faith in this at all and thought it would be much better to push on towards safety whilst they could. However, the small ship with us, which had key personnel on board, was apparently having engine trouble. Food was in very short supply and all we had were some biscuits and a drop of water.

71

About 8 a.m. a Japanese plane came over. It had obviously spotted us as it circled round and then went off. The Principal Matron had been given a cabin and she was having a conference with the other three Matrons. About mid-day a number of Japanese bombers appeared and bombed both of the ships and the island of Pompong. I was then on the lower deck talking to my own Matron, Miss Russell. The *Kuala* received a direct hit which killed the other three Matrons and caused a great many casualties. The ship was on fire and everyone was ordered up on deck and told to jump into the water. I had no lifejacket. I was wearing my one-piece grey dress with just under-garments underneath, my shoes and stockings and my tin hat. Some man took off my tin hat as I jumped into the sea, which was a helpful and kindly act, but I still had my shoes on. I went down very deep and got rid of my shoes as soon as I came up. Miss Russell, who was supposed to be a very strong swimmer, jumped with me but I never saw her again. The sea was covered with dead, dying and swimming people. The Japanese planes came over four times, dive-bombing the *Kuala* and machine-gunning the swimmers. I dived deep every time they came over. The water was green and calm and quite warm. The cries of the wounded and the drowning were heart-breaking. The *Kuala* was gradually sinking as the planes at last departed and the *Tien Kwang* was part-submerged.

The island was not far away but the swirling currents made the swim there a difficult one—particularly without a lifebelt. However, I stuck to my line and after great difficulty reached the island and was hauled out quite exhausted by the men who had been on the island collecting camouflage. They had also been bombed and several of them had been killed and wounded.

Sister Gwen Dowling from East Ballina, New South Wales, Australia (an Australian Sister who had been at Dunkirk), writes:

Sister Brenda Wells jumped off the *Kuala* with me and swam strongly to start with but must have been caught by the

73

machine-gun fire, as she suddenly disappeared. I found my hand caught in the hair of a dead Chinese girl who had lost one of her legs. I went with the current, diving down when the planes came over. I was fully clothed when I went into the water, wearing my tin hat, full uniform, shoes and stockings, and someone had given me a lifebelt. I thought I was alone but I was joined by a Canadian Sister called Charmian, who was clad only in her underclothes. We saw a lifeboat full of women, with two men rowing. Sister Black of our No. 17 Hospital called to me to say that the men were exhausted and could we help. We got into the boat and Charmian and I rowed it across to the southern beach of Pompong Island, where I was later joined by Margot Turner.

Other survivors from the *Kuala* took refuge on one or other of the islets which dotted the Straits. They received much help from friendly Chinese. The luckier ones were later picked up by British Naval vessels. Others who were not so lucky fell into the hands of the Japanese. But, as it turned out, the unluckiest of all were the large contingent of some two hundred and fifty—mostly women and children—who had taken refuge on Pompong Island. Before the two ships sank to the bottom, however, they managed to salvage some food and medical supplies—which subsequently saved their lives for a time at least.

Margot Turner again takes up the tale:

There were seven QAs with me—Sisters Pedlow, Tombs, Fowler, Le Blanc Smith, Black, Cooper and Strachan. A Naval officer on the beach told us that there were other survivors on the far side of Pompong; they had found a spring of fresh water in a clearing there and they proposed to make this their camp and a collecting place for the sick and wounded. The others all went over there but I was still exhausted and kept feeling a bit faint. I was also attending to a very badly wounded young British soldier so I decided I would just stay put for the time being. He had been hit by a bomb splinter and was unconscious. I stayed with him until he died. I never discovered his name. I slipped his body into the sea and wondered what I was going to do next.

The *Kuala* had now sunk but the *Tien Kwang*, though probably settled on the bottom, was still partly visible. The Naval officer came along and persuaded me to take shelter behind some rocks as the Japanese bombers were coming over again. This time, however, they left the island alone, except for some machine-gunning as they left, and concentrated on finishing off the *Tien Kwang*. I was still feeling rather groggy but he helped me scramble round the outskirts of Pompong and, with a little swimming, we joined the others. I really felt all in but there was plenty of work for me and the other Sisters to do as the many wounded and sick needed all our attention. The Sisters tore strips off their already rather tattered dresses to make bandages. We were all rationed to one biscuit and half a mug of water a day. The Sisters cut branches to make their patients as comfortable as possible. Our medical supplies were few and very precious; but at least we had some morphia which made the last hours of the mortally wounded more bearable. Many of them were past recovery. There was no medical officer but the Sisters divided themselves into shifts. I soon reacted to the urgency of the situation and became my own self again.

For three days this routine continued; and then, in the middle of the night, a small cargo steamer, which traded between the islands, put in. Its name was the *Tanjong Penang*. Between two hundred and fifty and three hundred women and children were loaded aboard her, plus wounded men and survivors whom she had already picked up from the wrecks of other ships. In view of the number of sick and wounded the captain asked if he could have some of the nurses and Margot was one of those who went aboard, the remains of her filthy borrowed grey dress hanging on her and her dark brown hair a tangled mess around her drawn and haggard face.

It was decided that the nurses off duty were to go and those on duty were to stay with such wounded and sick who could not be moved. It appeared at the time that those who went would probably survive and that the ones left behind faced almost certain death. But fate decided otherwise. Margot was the only one of the former who survived but quite a few of the latter were taken off later and many even escaped the horrors of a Japanese prison camp. Generally speaking the people who sought to escape in ships were sunk or captured and those who managed to find native craft or small launches escaped.

Gwen Dowling was one of the Sisters left behind on Pompong when the *Tanjong Penang* left with Margot Turner on board. Gwen had been sure that one of the many bodies she saw there floating in the water was that of Sister Brenda Wells but she was too exhausted to wade out and make certain.

Gwen continues her narrative:

After another three days a small motor boat with an Australian and two Malays arrived and said they would ship all the remaining wounded, and the women who were left, provided that a Sister went with them. I volunteered to go. We eventually arrived at Tambilihan on the Indragiri River in Sumatra. There were fifteen badly wounded, Matron Spedding being one of them, and forty or fifty others. At Tambilihan there was a Dutch dispensary and the Dutch District Officer gave us food and necessities. The boat which took us off Pompong Island returned there and brought off the remaining people. A small, well-trained group of Australian Navy men later took her back to Singapore Harbour to sink Japanese ships by putting limpet mines on the hulls. It was so successful that it was tried a second time but the diver was caught and beheaded. The rest of the crew escaped. This little boat, which is called the *Krait*, now has a place of honour in Sydney Harbour.

The escape route from Tambilihan was up the River Indragiri and then over the mountains of Padang to the west coast of Sumatra. Two Australian officers and three Privates took me and another Sister in a small motor boat up the rushing river, which was almost too exciting. After a night in a school we were put in a train to Padang. There was here a large collection of refugees—mostly women. When the others arrived we were split into three groups. Our group was billeted in a Dutch Convent. At this stage, we five QAs could have gone south in a Military transport full of soldiers. This seemed a foolish idea to me but the Japanese were closing in from all directions and we were advised that we should get out whilst we could. However, just at the last moment a destroyer, the *Danae*, arrived at night to refuel and they took all the seven hundred refugees on board. There were two other Naval ships with her, the RN ship, *Dragon*, and the RAN ship, *Hobart*. My brother was captain of the latter when he met me at Melbourne in 1946. We zig-zagged successfully across the Indian Ocean to Colombo.

There, we five QAs were sent to work in the new Army Hospital. The Australian Red Cross were very good to us and fitted us out with clothes. We were then sent to various hospitals in India where we worked until the end of the war.

Well, what adventures they had; but how lucky they were compared with Margot Turner and all the unfortunates with her who had to endure three and a half ghastly years in Japanese hands—during which so many of them died.

Margot continues:

It was a nightmare getting all these people on the *Tanjong Penang* in the dark, but at least there were now a certain number of men who could help. There was a lady doctor, Mrs. Thompson, and Mrs. Stringer, wife of the Director of Medical Services, also the Matron of No. 12 CGH from Singapore and several of her Sisters. The lady doctor had her work cut out but all the QAs and a civilian nurse, Miss McPherson, lent a hand and were working full out from the time they got on board. The ship sailed early the next morning, 17 February. It seemed fantastic that it was only five days since we had left Singapore. I was kept busy most of the day rationing out the food and water and helping with the dressings for the wounded. To give the Sisters a bath the captain turned the hose on us, after which I put my grey dress—or what was left of it—back on again. All the women and children and the patients were down below in the hold.

As a reward for all our hard work the captain allowed the nurses to sleep on deck. We had hardly settled down when, about 9 p.m., a searchlight blazed down on us and, without any warning, there were two violent explosions as two shells hit the ship. I was lying next to Sister Beatrice Le Blanc Smith and there were people dead and dying all round us. Beatrice got a nasty wound in the buttock which she said nothing about at the time. The ship was a ghastly shambles of mutilated bodies. My first thought was for the women and children in the hold; but a VAD, struggling up from there to the deck, her dress covered with blood, said that the hold had had the full force of one of the shells and was absolutely smashed. In any case I realized that there was nothing I could do as the ship was already at a steep angle and obviously just about to turn over. Beatrice and I just stepped into the sea and were very lucky not to be sucked down when the ship suddenly turned over and sank. This time, however, I had been taking no chances and had gone to bed in my lifejacket.

Just before the ship went down the ship's officers had managed to throw a few small rafts overboard and Beatrice and I got hold of two of these and tied them together. This sinking was much worse than the *Kuala*; the cries and screams of the wounded, the helpless and the dying, were quite terrible; and the fact that it was in the middle of the night made it all so much worse. Dead bodies and debris from the ship were floating everywhere. During the night we two Sisters swam around and managed to pick up fourteen people, including six children, two of whom were under one year old. There was room for two people to sit back to back on each raft, each one of them holding a child in their lap. The rest of them were in the water hanging on to the lifelines. I instilled into all of them the importance of never letting go; but when dawn broke I found that two of them had gone.

The captain of the *Tanjong Penang* hailed us from one of the ship's lifeboats but he said it was stove in and already leaking badly. He said that if he didn't sink he would try to get help. He told me to cling on and not give up hope— perhaps a Dutch plane would fly over. We never saw him again.

Beatrice, who had insisted on being one of those in the water, looked so ghastly that I hauled her on to the raft and found she had a desperate wound. She died that afternoon—as bravely as she had lived.*

The tropical sun was beating down on us and, despite my efforts to hold them, two more of the women let go and were carried away. There was only one other person on the raft whom I had ever met before, when she was in Alexandra Hospital in Singapore. She died at the end of the first day; and on the second day the

*The last letter received from Sister B. Le Blanc Smith, QAIMNS, 1st Malaya General Hospital, by her father and mother, was dated 1 January 1942, and was received by them in England on 1 May 1942, two and a half months after her death. It ran as follows:

Don't worry about me. Whatever happens to me cannot but be for the best and whatever I may have to go through is all experience and proves one's strength of character and fundamental beliefs. I have no fear for myself and look on life as a great adventure with the unexpected round every corner. Many people, finding themselves left with nothing, are learning life's true values, perhaps for the first time. To hold life cheaply, and all one's worldly possessions of no account, takes some doing but it is the lesson many have to learn, and until one experiences it, it is impossible to forecast one's reactions. Waiting for the baptism of fire doesn't worry me much except for the usual empty feeling at the sound of planes and guns. One Sister here has been through France, the Middle East and Greece—and I want to do likewise. At last my existence here seems about to be justified and the children went mad. We had a terrible time with them—and lost them all. I examined each of them with great care before committing their small bodies to the sea. The last one was a very small baby and it was difficult to know when it was dead. I thought, "This is some woman's precious child; I must not let it go until I know it's dead." But in the end there was no doubt and it had to go with the others. One by

---

year of "fun and games" preceding this was just the prelude and will be something to be remembered with a tolerant smile.

There had been rumours that she was a prisoner of war and that, and other rumours, caused the Matron-in-Chief QAIMNS from the War Office in Curzon Street, to issue this note: "It is not War Office policy to encourage the next of kin of missing personnel in the Far East to entertain much hope that their relatives are alive; the grim facts of the Far East situation make it most unlikely that any large proportion of them have survived and it is no kindness to raise false hopes."

Having been allowed to read the correspondence files of the Matron-in-Chief I was much moved by the number of anxious letters from relatives of QAs after the fall of Singapore—amongst them Margot Turner's mother—asking the ever-insistent and poignant question: "What has happened to my daughter?"

The photo of Beatrice with a patient was taken in Singapore in December 1941 and was eventually returned to her parents by the War Office, with her effects.

one the other women had gone and on the second night, 19 February, I was left alone with a Mrs. Barnett, whom I had never seen before, but felt that at least I should know her name.

As we could now see no single soul on the face of the ocean we decided to let one raft go and both sit back to back on the other one with our feet in the water. Our lifejackets had made our chins absolutely raw so we took them off and tied them at the side of the raft so that they trailed in the water. It was our third afternoon on the raft (20 February) and we could now see a number of little islands round about; but the currents were terrible and we didn't know how we could possibly reach any of them. We managed to catch two pieces of driftwood and with these we began to paddle feebly towards one of the islands. Mrs. Barnett let her paddle slip from her grasp and, before I could stop her, she had plunged into the sea after it, clutching the two lifejackets with her as she went. I was much too weak to swim after her. I called and strained my eyes to catch sight of her—but there was just nothing. I was now all alone.

It was at this moment that I became acutely conscious of the will to live. I was determined that I would hold on to life as long as it was humanly possible. I prayed that help would come and felt very definitely that some unseen power was watching over me. Why me, and not those others who had drifted away? I managed to collect a few drops of rain-water in the lid of my powder compact and also ate some seaweed which floated near the raft. Night came and I watched the stars and soaked up the rain that beat down on me. I thought of home and my family and the happy things in my life.

Although Margot was to face other very grim ordeals as a prisoner of the Japanese this present one was the greatest crisis of her life and the sternest test of her character. There were several qualities which helped to pull her through. First—and most important perhaps—was the self-discipline which had been instilled into her since the first day she had joined St. Bartholomew's Hospital. She knew that in an emergency any sign of panic or surrender on her part would show in her face and lower the morale of those whom it was her duty to encourage and support. And at this moment, when she had no one else to worry about but herself, she knew that any feeling of despair or hopelessness would lower her ability to hang on and keep alive. There was also her medical knowledge which made her aware that the mental controls the physical and if the mind loses control then all is lost. In the case of the other people on the raft—except for Sister Le Blanc Smith, whose wound was so grievous that it dominated all else—it was the will to live which had broken first. Margot knew quite well that if she "let go" mentally in her exhausted physical state she would fall into a doze, or even a coma, and slip off the raft to her death. So she kept saying her prayers to God—kept thinking of her home and her friends—kept thinking of anything that would take her mind away from the rapidly weakening state of her body.

Suddenly, in the afternoon of the fourth day, whilst she was still clinging to life, she saw a ship appearing over the horizon. It mattered not what sort of a ship it was—the agonizing question was whether it would continue to come in her direction—whether it would see her on the small raft—and if it did would it take any notice? She wasn't strong enough to stand up and wave, but at least she could sit up to show that she was still alive. When she looked down at herself she realized that she was burnt black by the sun and must look like a Malay woman.

As the ship came closer she saw that it was a battleship and hoped against hope that it might be British. As it approached her the ship slowed down and she could see all the little yellow faces peering over the side—and knew for certain what she had feared. It was Japanese.

A rope was thrown down to her and she was told to tie it round her waist; but she was much too weak to do this, so one of the sailors came down a rope ladder, tied the rope round her and she was hauled up the side as unceremoniously as a bale of cargo.

Margot continues:

Fortunately for me there was a doctor on board who had been trained in America and could speak English. He also knew the sort of condition I was in and that, although I was almost raving with thirst, it would be death for me to drink too much too soon. They put a piece of matting down on the deck for me under an awning, gave me some tea and a little drop of whisky and then some bread and milk. The grey dress, what was left of it, had disappeared; I thought it had probably come off whilst I was being hauled on board. They gave me a shirt and some trousers, tended my painful sunburns, and let me alone to rest and recover and go to sleep. Later they questioned me and asked who I was, where I had come from and where I was going. I told them that I was a QA from Singapore—and where I had been going to I hadn't the faintest idea. Late that night they roused me and said that they were going into harbour and I would be put ashore. The doctor told me that the harbour was Muntok on the Dutch East Indies island of Banka, off Sumatra.

When the ship had anchored, they told me to get up but I was quite unable to walk and the doctor and one of the sailors carried me down the gangway on to a long pier. To my astonishment I heard English voices hailing me. They were British prisoners of war working under Japanese supervision. They crowded round and offered me some tinned peaches. But after one mouthful I could eat no more. They wanted to carry me down the pier themselves but were told to get on with their work and the Japanese doctor carried me himself. At the end of the pier I was put on a stretcher and borne off to the civilian prisoners' camp. There, some civilian Nursing Sisters took charge of me.

The camp consisted of about eight huts with concrete floors, no furniture and an open square in the centre. It had previously been used to house two hundred Chinese coolies and now held six hundred to seven hundred British Servicemen and civilian men, women and children. The Japanese battleship remained four days in Muntok harbour and the doctor came to visit me every day and was extremely kind. Lo and behold, one day he arrived with the remains of my grey dress, cleaned, pressed and on a hanger!

The date was 21 February. It was unbelievable, when I looked back, that only nine days had elapsed since I left Singapore. And in that short time I had experienced such awful catastrophes and seen so much death and suffering. To anyone who has not experienced the sudden destruction of a ship at sea, crammed full of women and children, with no lifeboats, and lifejackets only for the very few, it is difficult to imagine the sheer ghastliness of the scene. And if on top of all this there is machine-gunning of helpless people in the water, and the darkness of night, it becomes all the more horrible. Those who left the ship alive simply didn't know what to do—or who to try to help; and the wailing of helpless mothers looking for their children, and vice versa, is a sound the survivors are never likely to forget.

One curious thing about all these sinkings in the Java Sea is that no one mentioned the danger from sharks, whereas in the Indian Ocean, they were a real menace to shipwrecked mariners. That there were plenty of sharks, in the Java Sea, however, was evident when some of the Sisters saw thirteen of them laid out in the sun to dry on Banka Island.

Margot found that there were a number of

Australian Sisters in the camp, some British and Dutch civilian nurses and two QAs —Mary Cooper and a Mrs. Molly Watts Carter. It was interesting for her to compare notes with the survivors from two of the other ships, the *Vyner Brooke* and the *Mata Hari*, which had left Singapore on 12 and 13 February. The Australian Sisters had sailed in the *Vyner Brooke*. They also had refused to leave their patients in 2/10th Australian General Hospital and had finally been ordered to do so. They had been told to rendezvous in St. Andrew's Cathedral, where they were joined by the remaining Sisters of the 13th AGH and the 2/4th Casualty Clearing Station. This brought the total number of Australian nurses to sixty-five. The *Vyner Brooke* was a small, grey ship, flying a White Ensign. There were two hundred people on board, far too many for so small a boat. They were told that the sailing plan was to hide by day amongst the little islands and make as much progress towards Java as possible by night. But they were machine-gunned by a Japanese aircraft before they ever left Singapore harbour and all the lifeboats on the starboard side of the ship were holed.

Next day, at about 11 o'clock in the morning, the air raid signal blared out and all passengers were ordered on to the lower deck, where they lay crammed together like sardines, wearing their tin hats and lifebelts. The portholes were tightly closed and all they could hear was the droning of the planes. The *Vyner Brooke* carried one gun which now came into action. The first salvo of bombs missed as the ship took avoiding action and zig-zagged violently. Back came the planes again and this time one bomb hit the bridge and another went straight down the funnel and exploded in the engine room. Once more the planes came over and scored another direct hit on the ship, which was now on fire and sinking rapidly. But the planes had not finished with them yet and this time, on a low level run, they machine-gunned the deck and the lifeboats.

The ship was now listing heavily. The oldest people and the wounded were put into a lifeboat with Matron Drummond and one or two Sisters carrying first aid equipment; one other boat was launched successfully but others appeared to be too badly holed. Most of the wounded passengers jumped into the water as the *Vyner Brooke* slipped rapidly from sight, within fifteen minutes of the first bomb hit. Nothing remained except a pair of leaky boats, a few rafts, scattered wreckage and a lot of human heads bobbing on an oily sea

The Australian Sisters kept together, encouraging one another. Fortunately there were quite a number of rafts and bits of wreckage to which people were clinging. The Sisters all had morphia and field dressings with them and those who had managed to hang on to these medical aids were able to help the wounded. The strong tides, however, carried them in different directions; and though they kept seeing ships and boats no one appeared to take any notice. Finally some large motor boats, packed with Japanese soldiers, surrounded them, gave them a hard look—and passed on.

Somehow the night came, and passed, leaving them cold and miserable. They thanked Heaven for their lifebelts, though these rubbed their chins raw. When morning came they discovered that they had got mixed up with the Japanese occupation of Sumatra and there were transports and landing-craft everywhere. They had now drifted close inshore and were eventually carried into a river estuary and so ashore.

It was Tuesday the 17th and they had been in the water, or on a raft, or swimming, since Saturday. Some landed straight in the hands of the Japanese, others fell in with friendly Chinese who told them that they were on Banka Island and that there were some more white people in the prison camp at Muntok, which was where they were all eventually taken.

When the bulk of the Australian Sisters surviving from the *Vyner Brooke* arrived at Muntok they found that others of their number had landed at different piers and beaches and had different stories to tell. All of them were now clad in every sort of weird garment and they looked a very motley crowd. Out of the sixty-five Sisters who had been aboard the *Vyner Brooke* they could only muster thirty-one and they began to wonder what had happened to the other thirty-four, but hoped that they had managed to land on another part of the coast.

Meanwhile, to return to Margot Turner's own story. She relates:

About a week later another Australian, Sister Vivian Bullwinkel, arrived— and it was hoped that she might be able to give news of some of the others. She walked quietly in through the door of the jail, clasping an army water bottle to her side. We could see at once why she was doing this—it was to hide a bullet hole in her uniform. She had a most terrible tale to tell. With twenty-one other Australian Army Nursing Sisters and a group of Servicemen and civilian women she had reached the shore, some of them in one of the leaking lifeboats, at a beach about two or three miles from Muntok. They spent the first night sitting round a fire and then, next morning, as some of the men were wounded, they went in search of someone who might be able to care for them. However, they could find no one all that day and spent another night on the beach. Next morning a Naval officer volunteered to go off to try to get some stretchers and some food—and the civilian women went off on their own to find help.

The Australian Sisters, with Matron Drummond of the 13th AGH in charge, stayed to look after the wounded. A little later the Naval officer returned, bringing a party of Japanese soldiers with him. The Japanese separated from the Sisters all the men who could walk and took them along the beach round a promontory. After a little while the Japanese came back, wiping the blood off their bayonets. They then formed the nurses and the wounded into line, told them to walk into the sea, and machine-gunned them from the back.

All were killed except Vivian who was shot through the body and left floating unconscious in the water. When the Japanese had gone she struggled ashore. She wandered into the jungle and went to sleep. Next day she came across an English Serviceman who was one of those who had been bayoneted. He was very badly wounded and Vivian stayed with him for several days, going each day to a native village to get food and water for him. The natives were too frightened of the Japanese to help them further, but they told Vivian about the prison camp at Muntok and how to get there. A Japanese Naval officer picked them up in a car and took them to the jail. The British Serviceman died a few days later. What a terrible ordeal for Vivian Bullwinkel, a young Sister in her early twenties; and what tremendous courage she had shown.

We decided in the camp that we would never mention this incident as, if it got to the ears of the Japs, Vivian's life might have been in danger.

There is, however, a sequel to this story which I only uncovered whilst I was writing this book, with the help of Denis Russell-Roberts and Stoker Lloyd, RN, who told me the story, and of Vivian Bullwinkel herself. In addition to Vivian Bullwinkel and the English Serviceman (Private Kingsley) whom she nursed for ten days, and who eventually died of his wounds in the camp, there were in fact two other survivors of the massacre on the Banka Island beach and both of them arrived in Margot's camp hospital about the same time as did Vivian Bullwinkel. One was an American citizen from Singapore, whose name was H. McDougall, Jnr, who had also been a passenger on the *Vyner Brooke*. He had been shot and bayoneted and left for dead, but survived his years of imprisonment. The other was Stoker E. A. Lloyd, RN, who told his story to me as follows:

I arrived in Singapore in December 1941 and was mostly in and around Singapore Island during the operations but on several occasions was driving a Naval lorry up country on the mainland, taking supplies to Navy personnel and later bringing Naval personnel into Singapore from outlying gun positions to the Union Jack Club, where they had to assemble prior to evacuation. I embarked in *Vyner Brooke*, with other Navy and Army personnel, Australian nurses and women and children.

After the sinking of the ship I found myself in one of the only two serviceable lifeboats, which had been badly smashed and was riding on the air tanks and only just afloat. In addition to the full load of people we had in the boat we got hold of two rafts and tied them on to the stern of the boat and picked up as many people as we could, including a woman with a very small baby. It was very hard work as I and two others were the only people fit to do any rowing. The others were all women and children or wounded men—and also there was a strong current pulling us away from Banka Island, which we could see in the distance. It was nearly dark before we got there. Survivors from other ships had arrived on the main beach and were lighting fires to guide other people to it.

During the night more people kept arriving in ones and twos until there were well over fifty—a mixture of Servicemen and civilians, women and children, and a number of Australian Nursing Sisters. Many of them were wounded and some died during the night. We had very little to eat except hard ship's biscuits and tins of condensed milk which had been washed ashore from the wrecks of ships in the area.

I am not sure how many days went by before we saw the invasion fleet coming to Banka. At first we thought they were our ships but when we saw the Rising Sun flag our hearts fell.

The ship's officers then held a meeting and they decided that one officer should go to Muntok and surrender because our position was quite hopeless. It was also decided that a small party of the very elderly, sick and wounded should start walking slowly towards Muntok—and most of them got through.

The Naval officer arrived back with a party of Japanese soldiers under an officer. They first separated the men from the women and marched us up the beach towards Muntok until we came to a small bay with large rocks at the entrance. They then lined us all up at the water's edge, facing the sea. Until then I hadn't any idea what was about to happen. But then a Japanese officer went up to one man who was wearing a shirt and told him to take it off and tear it into strips to put over our eyes. The soldier refused to do this and the officer drew his sword and slashed him very severely across the face. We knew then all right what was going to happen. The man next to me, who was a seaman I had known in Singapore—I think his name was Jock McGlurk or something of the sort, but I always knew him as Jock—said, "This is where you get it, Ernie, right in the back."

I said, "Not for me, Jock," and we both dived into the sea, with one other man, as the Japs opened fire with a machine-gun.

They mowed down the others first and then turned the gun on the three of us. I was a powerful swimmer and was going well. Jock cried out, "I'm hit, Ernie," and both he and the other man sank out of sight. I then got the Japs' undivided attention—and they weren't going to leave anyone alive. I saw a bullet hit the water at my side and then felt a bullet hit my head and I thought it had gone right through; but in actual fact it only grazed my scalp. Then another bullet went right through my left shoulder and leg. I must have looked—and certainly felt—a dead man as I floated half submerged round the rocks, was washed up on a bit of sand, and lost consciousness.

When I came to it was dark; my head and shoulder throbbed and it was raining. The next day I started to look for food and luckily found some coconuts and a fresh-water stream. I lay like this for a few days and then thought I ought to walk back along the beach to see if any of the others had survived.

It was quite horrible. All the male bodies had been piled on top of one another in one big heap. Then I went farther along and found the bodies of the Australian nurses and other women. They lay at intervals of a few yards—in different positions and in various stages of undress. They had been shot and then bayoneted. It was a shocking sight.

I roamed about for a few more days and then decided to walk towards Muntok and give myself up. I narrowly escaped being shot by the first Japanese who captured me but eventually arrived at the camp and was thankful to get into hospital and have my wounds attended to. Later Vivian Bullwinkel came to see me as the man she had looked after for ten days on the beach was in the next bed to me. He had been very badly wounded and he died in a few days.* Vivian and I talked about our lucky escape from the massacre but agreed that we wouldn't say too much about it as, if the Japs knew, our lives would not be worth a moment's purchase.

*Vivian Bullwinkel tells me (on 19.8.1969) that when she was in England in 1950 she corresponded with Private Kingsley's wife, who had since re-married.

Stoker Lloyd was a very tough man; he recovered from his wounds and survived three years of prison camp brutality before being repatriated to England, where he served the last two years of his term of service. He was in South Africa from 1948 to 1960, married a South African girl and, at the time of writing, he works in the Spencer Steel Works at Newport, Wales.

His story is just another illustration of Japanese ruthlessness. This was not a case of killing prisoners in the heat of battle, but cold-blooded murder, when they knew that the prison camp was only a few miles away. Perhaps General Percival was right after all to get the Sisters out of Singapore before the Japanese got there.

5

Muntok Internment Camp

THE coastal steamer, *Mata Hari*, left Singapore at 10 p.m. on 12 February —the day before the *Kuala*. Captain A. C. Carston, RNVR had orders to proceed to Batavia via the Durian and Banka Straits, taking all possible cover from enemy aircraft during the hours of daylight. His ship carried one 4-inch gun astern. They left with well over 300 passengers on board and then, just after the ship had weighed anchor, were asked to take on board another 120, which made a total of 483 people aboard, including the ship's officers and crew. Every inch of deck space was taken up.

Amongst them was Christine Bundy who had been working at one of the Medical Services First Aid Posts in Singapore for the past ten months. It was on the *Mata Hari* that she met Norman Cleveley, whom she married after the war. There were also Valda Godley, whose husband was on military

106

duty in Singapore, and Ruth Russell-Roberts. Ruth's husband, Denis, was serving with the 3/11th Sikh Regiment in Malaya. The Russell-Robertses had a baby daughter called Lynette. Whilst Denis was in action with his battalion up country, Ruth had taken a job in Malayan Command. Just before Christmas, however, she sent Lynette home to her sister in England in the care of a friend; but she herself was determined to stay at her job, particularly when Denis was reported missing. Fortunately, he turned up safe and sound a few weeks later and this made it easier for her to go when she, with the other British women, was ordered to leave Singapore. Denis got a few hours' leave to see her off. They were never to meet again.

As with the other "little ships" there were acute problems with regard to the rationing of food and water and, perhaps most difficult of all, the organization of washing and sanitary facilities. For the use of the officers there were only three European-type WCS, and a dozen Asiatic-type pans for the use of the crew. The WCS were allotted to the women and the men had to share the remaining facilities. What would have happened in this respect if their voyage had not been brought to an abrupt conclusion is nobody's business.

The captain decided to anchor in the Durian Straits early the next morning, as close inshore as possible, where his ship, with luck, would not be seen. The anchor had scarcely been lowered, however, when a flight of nine Japanese bombers appeared, flying quite high. They spotted the ship and dropped six bombs but did not achieve any direct hits, although the bombs threw up great fountains of water. Whether they thought that the ship had been effectively crippled or whether they had urgent work elsewhere, the Jap aircraft kept steadily on their course. The captain then moved the *Mata Hari* to another more sheltered anchorage. But they were kept on the alert all day as flight after flight of Japanese planes kept passing over.

In the late afternoon the voyage was continued with no further alarms; and then, at 9 p.m., they saw some gun flashes which could only have come from warships in action. The captain decided to proceed with all possible speed until dawn and then seek cover in the Tochjoch Islands. At about one o'clock in the morning of Saturday 14 February they were hailed from the darkness by English voices and picked up six swimmers, two Naval officers and four ratings, from HMS *Scorpion*, which had been sunk by a Japanese cruiser. They had been swimming for six hours and reckoned they were the only survivors. The *Scorpion* had been a Yangtse River gunboat before becoming part of the Malayan Auxiliary Fleet. She had received considerable bomb damage in Malaya and had left Singapore a couple of days before the *Mata Hari*. Badly in need of repairs, she was limping slowly towards Batavia, when a Japanese cruiser, accompanied by two destroyers, was sighted. The *Scorpion* immediately engaged the three ships and in the ensuing action was sunk.

Captain Carston had also received information that HMS *Giang Bee* had been sunk—probably by the same Japanese ships. Many women and children were amongst the *Giang Bee*'s passengers, of whom only a total of seventy survived. Carston decided to head the *Mata Hari* for the coast of Sumatra, keeping as close inshore as possible so that, if the ship was engaged by enemy naval craft, the passengers might have a chance of swimming to safety. As the Japanese warships were obviously shooting on sight the captain considered that it would probably be advisable for him to land his passengers at any convenient Dutch port rather than risk their being sunk at sea. With all the passengers safely out of harm's way, the *Mata Hari* would then be able to proceed with unrestricted freedom of action. Such was the captain's plan, which didn't quite work out as intended.

At first light the *Mata Hari* entered Sukanah Bay, which was situated about twenty miles north of the entrance to the Moesi River and roughly seventy miles overland from Palembang. As they entered the bay there was a deafening sound of aircraft overhead, a formation of eighty-one big Japanese bombers and twenty Zero fighters. But, apart from firing a volley of machine-gun fire, this air armada continued on in the direction of Sumatra. The *Mata Hari* proceeded deep into Sukanah Bay and there dropped anchor.

They up-anchored in the evening allowing sufficient time to make their way out of the bay in daylight. They arrived off the mouth of the Moesi River about 8 p.m. and with Palembang only seventy miles up the river, it began to look as though the passengers' anxieties might soon be over. But, unknown to them, a battle was being fought at Palembang and the Japanese air armada, which had passed over them, had carried paratroops who had been dropped around the town and the oil refineries. Carston of course knew nothing of this and continued with his plan to land his passengers at Palembang; but he could not proceed up the river without a pilot and all efforts to obtain one were unavailing.

Suddenly they saw searchlights and heard gunfire out in Banka Strait and it appeared that some sort of naval action was taking place and was coming closer. Carston had only two alternatives—the safest would have been to take refuge up the Moesi River, but without a pilot, that was not practicable. He therefore had to take the second alternative—to put to sea and try to escape under cover of darkness. As captain of a King's ship, flying the White Ensign, it was his duty to fight to the last; but on the other hand, with so many women and children on board, he knew he could not expose them to the horrors of a naval engagement. Having reached that decision he gave orders to his officers that, if intercepted, they would strike the White Ensign and not offer any resistance.

All the shipping was blacked out and they played a game of blind man's buff all night with a number of hostile vessels all about them. Then, at 3 a.m., when they seemed to have left all the trouble behind, a searchlight opened full on them. In International Code they were ordered to anchor at once and show a light. At least they had come off better than the *Kuala*, the *Tanjong Penang* and the *Vyner Brooke*.

It was Sunday 15 February—the day of the Singapore surrender. The morning light revealed a Japanese cruiser a thousand yards away, which then steamed slowly round them with all guns trained. At that moment there suddenly appeared a big British Naval launch, HM Motor Launch *311*, commanded by Lieutenant Christmas of the Royal New Zealand Volunteer Reserve. Leaving Singapore on the night of 13 February, with a crew of fifteen, and fifty-seven Service passengers aboard, she too was bound for

Batavia. The Japanese cruiser opened fire on the launch as did two destroyers which raced up to join in the battle. Armed only with one three-pounder gun and three machine-guns, *311* was magnificently handled. Twisting and turning like a hare to avoid the hail of shells, she closed the range to less than a thousand yards in order to bring her little gun into play.

The passengers on the *Mata Hari* watched this heroic but hopeless action with bated breath, praying that the gallant little launch might somehow escape. But the end soon came and *311* went down with her colours still flying. No one will ever know of the many other gallant episodes such as this in these waters, where small units of British resistance fought it out to the last with the overpowering might of Japan.

The Japanese cruiser then sent a boat across to the *Mata Hari* with a boarding party. The Japanese ratings scattered over the ship and took charge of the bridge, engine-room and wireless-room. The *Mata Hari*'s anchor was hove to and she proceeded back to the small port of Muntok, where, just before midnight, Japanese troops had made a seaborne landing. The narrow waters of Banka Strait must have been swarming with Japanese craft that night. In spite of this the *Mata Hari* had managed to slip through the whole armada —until the last ship had trapped her.

All the men aboard the *Mata Hari* were landed, with the Japanese boarding party as escort. Now that the *Mata Hari*'s voyage was over, and the necessity for economy no longer existed, Captain Carston threw open the store-room so that his passengers could help themselves to whatever they fancied. Throughout the day huge trays of canned sausages were kept frying on the galley stove and opened tins of biscuits were placed on the decks.

At four o'clock that afternoon, the boats returned to take the women and children ashore. But at least they had had one good meal, the last they were to get for three and a half years—those of them who survived that long. They were landed at Muntok pier, where Margot Turner was to be landed a few days later, a long line of struggling people, each one loaded with just what they could carry. This pier was in fact five hundred and fifty yards long—the longest pier that any of them had ever seen—and it seemed much longer to these burdened people. They spent that night huddled together on the pier itself; and during the night Japanese soldiers walked among them, jeering and laughing at their plight. There was no drinking water and no sanitation. Next morning they had another long and weary walk through the streets of Muntok and far beyond—until they reached the Coolie prisoners' camp. There they became part of the large gathering of civilian prisoners—the survivors of some sixty ships which had been sunk or captured in the vicinity of the Banka Straits —with whom Margot Turner was to share the next three and a half years of her life.

It says much for the toughness of Margot's constitution that she started to pick up her strength even on the starvation ration the Japs allowed them. She had always had a great antipathy to rice and when she was given her first meal in the camp, a small bowl of rice, she refused it. Her friends told her at once that she had better get to like it as she wouldn't receive anything else. In fact their food consisted of two rice meals a day, with sometimes a bit of dried octopus. So Margot faced up to her antipathy and, having first made herself eat rice with a good deal of difficulty, gradually came to like it—and that was one of the reasons why she survived her captivity whilst so many others succumbed. However, for the first few weeks in the camp she had to depend very much on the assistance of the other QA and civilian Sisters. Almost at once she was faced with a condition arising out of her ordeal on the raft which might well have proved fatal.

Margot recalls:

I began to get red patches on my legs which spread upwards and became very painful, keeping me awake at night. There was a naval doctor in the camp who had a look at them but could suggest nothing but an application of calamine. My legs got steadily worse and I realized perfectly well that I had some acute form of poisoning. One of the civilian Sisters, Mary McCullum (later Mrs Clark), who was looking after me, arranged for a Dr. Kerr to have a look at me. He was an elderly Scotsman, who had been practising in Singapore for a number of years. As soon as he had examined my legs he was quite convinced that I had deep-seated pus in both legs—what he called "seawater boils". They would have to be lanced at once and all he had to do it with was a blunt scalpel—and with this he opened up the patches and out poured the pus. Painful as these lancings were I realized quite well that they had saved my life. The kindly Dr. Kerr died afterwards in the men's camp.

The Muntok camp was terribly crowded and, on 2 March, the civilian men, women and children were moved across the Banka Straits and sixty miles up the Moesi River to Palembang in Sumatra. This was a most trying and uncomfortable journey—first by launch to a dirty old tramp steamer, and then up the Moesi River. They were alternately burnt by the sun and drenched by the rain, with no shelter, no sanitation and very little food or water. Nearing Palembang the river was thick with oil. There was a huge oilfield near by. Two ships had been sunk in the river which made the passage difficult. About twenty women stayed behind— mostly Sisters—to look after the sick, amongst whom was Margot Turner. More Service prisoners were then brought into the Muntok camp. The women and children were moved to Palembang in batches of about a hundred and fifty each week. Margot was in the last batch, which left on 1 April. She was taken on a stretcher to Palembang and there nursed for about a month in a hospital run by some Dutch nuns who were very good to her.

Margot recalls:

At Palembang the men were separated from the women and children, and as by this time the Dutch were interned also, the women's camp consisted of two thirds Dutch and one third British—about seven hundred in all. The women lived in small Dutch houses, very overcrowded, with about twenty-five to thirty-five in each. There was very little furniture, one double bedstead, quite bare, a few chairs and one small couch; but we were very thrilled to have an electric stove. The Dutch people from outside the camp were very helpful and kind; they called on three occasions, bringing hot soup, a few toothbrushes and odd things of which we were greatly in need. They also brought in bread, packs of cards, chess sets and some cushions, which were certainly a great luxury. These things were all done at great risk to the Dutch themselves. The rations also improved, thanks again to the Dutch people and their Malayan servants. We were given some green vegetables and a ration of pork on two occasions in our first month.

Of course we had barbed wire all round and Japanese soldiers to guard us. We had no hospital in this camp, but about two miles away was the Dutch hospital run by Roman Catholic nuns, who had not been interned and had been so very kind to me: and it was to them that the sick Service-men, civilian men, women and children, were sent. The hospital was always over-worked and understaffed and we trained nurses asked if we could go and help them. But the Japanese sternly refused.

In those early days we had no commu-nal cooking and we used to cook in small groups over terribly smoky fires which we had made ourselves. So, besides nursing, our work consisted of cooking (probably for about twelve people), and collecting the rations—which meant carrying sacks of rice and large logs of wood which had to be sawn and chopped before they could be used to light a fire. Looking back on those early days, they were in a sense luxury days of internment compared to what we had to put up with later. We had plenty of rice then, so were able to make all kinds of fancy dishes; we were also able to buy extra things such as sugar, fruit, coconuts, coffee and curry stuffs, which certainly helped the rice down. People who hadn't money, but had jewellery, could sell it for money. Others would work for other people to get money—chop wood, do washing, etc. As in ordinary life, so in camp, there were always people who had plenty (mostly Dutch) and those who had nothing. But I think, on the whole, those who had nothing were the happiest because they did not miss it so much when things got really bad.

We had more free time in those early days—bridge was played quite a lot, with home-made cards—also Mah Jong, for which a friend and I made a suitable set out of bits of wood. We had French and Malay classes and some more energetic people learnt Dutch; and we arranged concerts and debates, all of which helped us to forget. The only music that we had was written from memory by an English missionary—Miss Dryburgh. We also had a church service every Sunday morning, taken by one of the missionaries. Occasionally the Japs stopped it but the church service was about the only thing we were allowed to continue when the Japs stopped all concerts.

Margaret Dryburgh must have been nearly sixty and had for many years been doing missionary work in the Far East. She was a quiet, unassuming woman whom everybody loved. She played a major part, not only in organizing the concerts, but the church services also. She ran the Glee Club, helped to produce a camp magazine and wrote a wonderful "Captives' Hymn" which was sung for the first time in July 1942. Thenceforward it was sung every Sunday and proved a great inspiration to the prisoners. The hymn ran as follows:

Father in captivity
We would lift our prayer to Thee
Keep us ever in Thy love,
Grant that daily we may prove
Those that place their trust in Thee
More than conquerors may be.

Give us patience to endure
Keep our hearts serene and pure
Grant us courage, charity
Greater faith, humility
Readiness to own Thy will
Be we free or captive still.

For our country we would pray
In this hour be Thou our stay
Pride and selfishness forgive
Teach her by Thy laws to live
By Thy grace may all men see
That true greatness came from Thee.

For our loved ones we would pray
Be their guardian night and day
From all danger keep them free
Banish all anxiety.
May they trust us to Thy care
Know that Thou our pains dost share.

May the day of freedom dawn
Peace and Justice be reborn.
Grant that nations loving Thee
O'er the world may brothers be,
Cleansed by suffering, know rebirth
See Thy Kingdom come on earth.

The singing was wonderful, people of all creeds, colours and nationality joining in. There were about fifteen English women, including Miss Dryburgh, who were missionaries or mission teachers—and all of them were evacuees from Malaya or China. Miss Dryburgh died in April 1945.

The Japanese habit of "Tenko" or a count, without warning, was a most trying habit for us. We had to drop everything we were doing and stand out in the roadway, probably at the hottest part of the day, and wait to be counted. The senior prisoner in each group had to bow from the waist and give the number of prisoners in her group. The guard would then probably count it themselves several times over, getting a different answer each time and then discover that the original number given to them was correct. I found it very irksome and humiliating having to bow to the Japanese soldiers but I soon learnt my lesson at one of these "Tenkos" when I failed to do so and a Jap hit me in the face and knocked out one of my front teeth.

In August we were allowed to have a

"shop" in the camp. The shopkeeper was a Chinaman who brought in a bullock cart on Sundays, laden with various forms of fruit and a small amount of butter, tea and beans. This was fine for those who had money, but I had none.

In September the Japs asked for nurses to go and nurse at Pladjou oilfields hospital but they wouldn't be definite as to whether we would be nursing our own Allied nationals or Japanese and we were all a bit suspicious. Some weeks later they came into the open and said we would definitely be nursing Japanese. This had obvious dangers and we refused to go and were punished by having three of our houses taken away from us—just to make the overcrowding worse.

Three of the Dutch nurses were allowed to go and nurse in the Charitas Hospital in Palembang, about three miles from the camp. This hospital was run by Dutch nuns and doctors. It was a very small and awful place, packed with Allied Servicemen, civilian men and women. But we did use it as a means of communicating with some of the British and Australian patients.

Margot Turner had made the acquaintance of Ruth Russell-Roberts and her friends, Christine Bundy and Valda Godley. Margot says that "they were great friends and did everything together. Ruth was tall and slim and was mad on exercise. She was always walking, walking, walking. I still hear from Christine, who married again after the war. They were all three in the camp with us the whole time."

The story of Ruth and Denis Russell-Roberts, which is told so poignantly in the latter's book, *Spotlight on Singapore*, is typical of so many of the heartbreaks which occurred when wife and husband were parted and one of them—in this case both —were prisoners of the Japanese. And this was much the worst form of captivity anyone could undergo—if only because there were no available means of communication. The last spoken words that Ruth and Denis had together, as he saw her off on the *Mata Hari* on 13 February 1942, seemed afterwards to both of them so inadequate—but what more could they say? In that holocaust of bombing and fires, of death and of suffering, in which their happy and devoted life had come adrift, the chances of them ever continuing their married life with their baby daughter, Lynette, appeared very remote. And yet their sad story so very nearly had a happy ending.

Denis became a prisoner of war of the Japanese within forty-eight hours of their parting; but he was tough, and determined to remain alive—because he had so much to live for. On his way back from the docks to his regiment he passed the Indian General Hospital in Tyersall Park and saw the dreadful result of the Japanese bombing. More than two hundred helpless patients had been burnt to death; others were hobbling and crawling along Holland Road trying to make their way to the Civil Hospital in Singapore City.

Then dawned the fateful Sunday morning—15 February—the date of the surrender. With the departure of the last gallant RAF fighters the Japanese air domination of the sky was absolute. Towards evening came an uncanny silence which could only mean surrender. And early the next morning Denis Russell-Roberts's commanding officer read out a copy of General Percival's last message to his troops:

It has become necessary to give up the struggle, but I want the true reasons explained to all ranks. The forward troops continue to hold their ground, but the essentials of war have run short. In a few days we shall have neither food nor petrol and many types of ammunition are short, and the water supply, upon which the vast civil population, and many of the fighting forces, are dependent, threatens to fail. This situation has been brought about partly by being driven off the dumps and partly by hostile air and artillery action. Without these necessities of war we cannot carry on. I thank all ranks for their efforts throughout.

The General could well have added that the war in Malaya was lost in December when the modern aircraft promised to implement the plans for defence of Malaya and Singapore never arrived.

The 5/11th Sikhs fell in for the last time, with orders to march to Raffles Place where they were to hand over their arms to the Japanese. They marched by way of River Valley Road to avoid the horrors of Orchard Road where hundreds of mutilated bodies lay in heaps by the roadside. They scarcely saw any Japs. The Chinese and Malays kept indoors, few of them daring to venture forth. As they marched through Raffles Place the Indo-China Bank was flying the tricolour of Pétain's France. And then, after the Indian ranks had been separated from the British, Denis Russell-Roberts joined the long column of British officers and men marching to the Changi POW camp. The column presented a pathetic sight—led as it was by several files of Brigadiers and full Colonels, each laden with all his worldly possessions. As they passed Raffles Hotel a group of British women waved from an upstairs window and the troops had sufficient heart to sing "There'll always be an England". And so Denis and his fellows went into more than three years of bitter captivity from which ten thousand of them never returned.

It was some time in May that he first had news of Ruth from someone who had seen her in Palembang—and this was a tremendous relief to Denis in view of all the rumours regarding the sinking of the little ships in the Banka Straits and elsewhere. Now he wanted somehow to get a letter to her. As his fellow POWs were allowed to send a postcard (which hardly ever reached its destination) to their next-of-kin in the UK, he couldn't see why he couldn't send one to his wife at Palembang in Sumatra. But the Japs were quite adamant that there could be no communication between prisoners of war. At last Denis put his case to his Corps Commander, General "Piggy" Heath. But he had the same problem, as Lady Heath was even closer—in the women's portion of Changi Jail—and yet he was not allowed to communicate with her. Nearly three years after the war Denis went to stay with the Heaths at their home in Limuru, about ten miles outside Nairobi. Lady Heath, who had been a QA Nursing Sister herself, was then the proud mother of a young son. The General died a few years later, largely owing to the suffering inflicted on him by the Japanese.

Two and a half years were to pass before Ruth Russell-Roberts, in the same camp as Margot Turner, received news that her baby daughter, Lynette, had arrived safely in England. Ruth was a most splendid young woman, very slender, a fine athlete and always in top physical condition. The fact that she was very deaf somehow added to her attraction. She was also very determined and never gave up easily. Ever since the first months of her captivity Ruth had been trying to get a letter to Denis. Eventually she ascertained that if she could contact a Chinese by the name of Ah Wong, who sailed a junk to Singapore once a month, it might be possible to get him to take one. She learnt that Ah Wong was suffering from a poisoned foot and was attending once a week at the Charitas Hospital in Palembang, run by Dutch nuns and doctors. This was quite a small hospital with very primitive comforts for the patients, but it took in sick prisoners from the various camps and it was always full with Servicemen from the Mule School Camp and civilian prisoners from the jail. All the patients were kept under the strictest surveillance by Japanese guards who patrolled the corridors by day and night.

On Wednesday each week out-patients could visit the hospital. Ruth decided to develop toothache and managed to get taken from the women's camp in the ambulance. Whilst she was waiting in the passage for the Dutch dentist to arrive she managed to slip away to the lavatory which had a small outside window. By standing on tiptoe on the lavatory seat she was able to converse with one or two friendly Chinese outside. The result was that, at her third visit to the hospital, she managed to speak with Ah Wong, who was an elderly man with gold teeth and a warm smile. He told her that on the following Wednesday he would take her letter and give it to someone in Singapore who would take it to Changi.

In the last week of May 1942 Ah Wong set sail for Singapore, taking Ruth's letter with him. The letter reached Denis in Changi seven months later. He was standing beside the remains of one of the British 15-inch guns when someone thrust a soiled and crumpled envelope into his hands with just his name in pencil written on it. It told him all he wanted to know—that she was safe and well. Her last sentence was, "I live solely on the thought of being reunited with you and Lynette. Look after yourself, darling, don't worry about me. I can take it—Ruth."

6

Palembang—Imprisoned with Thieves and Murderers

MARGOT TURNER now had to make a decision which altered the monotonous tenor of her existence —but might have ended her life. The Sisters had asked many times if they could go and nurse in a hospital in which their own nationals were being treated; but any hospital, which was not for the Japanese, would have been better than nothing. Nursing was their profession. But the answer had always been "No".

However, at the beginning of October 1942, Margot recalls:

The Japanese officer in charge of the camp came in and asked to speak to four of us—two civilian Sisters, Mrs Olga Neubrunner and Miss Jennie Macalister (later Mrs Taylor), and the two QAs, Miss Mary Cooper and myself. He asked us if we

132

would like to go and nurse in a native hospital run by a Dutch doctor—Dr. Holweg who, before the war, had been head of the Red Cross in Palembang— and an Indonesian doctor—Dr. Gani. He told us that if we started nursing in this hospital, later we might be able to nurse our own people in the big hospital. We had no time to think it over; we had to make up our minds there and then and would leave the camp next day. So we all decided to go, hoping that in the end we would be able to nurse our own people. So, on 9 October 1942, we left the camp, sad to be leaving our friends and wondering what the future had in store for us.

The hospital was a converted school— with about a hundred beds—and our patients were Chinese and Malays. The staff consisted of the two doctors, the Dutch doctor living in the hospital, as we did. Then there was the Matron, Sister Emma, who was also a trained midwife, about six nurses, and some six male nurses—all Indonesians. In fact we had little to do with the latter as we worked independently. I was in charge of the theatre—a very primitive affair—but we managed to do quite a lot of operations, such as amputations, big abdominals, etc. The surgeon was a Dutch doctor called Teclecburg, who worked in the hospital where the POWs were and he used to bring the instruments and so on with him when he visited our hospital. He was a very good surgeon and a very charming person. Later he had a very bad time at the hands of the Japanese and has since died.

There was also a very big out-patient attendance. I used to work in this clinic and sometimes we had about two hundred people, mostly with terrible tropical ulcers—and of course we had very little medical equipment to deal with these. The work was interesting and I learnt a lot about tropical diseases. I also learnt to speak Malay, as only a very few of the patients could speak English, and it was a case of knowing the language in order to be understood.

On New Year's Eve Dr. Gani, the Indonesian doctor, invited the four of us nurses to a little party—about which we had to keep very quiet in front of the Japanese. An English dentist was also there. At midnight, to drink the New Year in, they gave us something in a wine glass which we subsequently discovered to be neat whisky. This was really kind of Dr. Gani as whisky must have been very precious.

We had been given passes and were allowed to go out to the town; but we normally only went if we wanted to do some shopping in the market. We were also allowed to visit the hospital where the POWs and internees were and we took full advantage of this as it meant we could take food and other things in to them and also do shopping for them and for the people in the camp. The guards always looked in our bags when we went in to the hospital and again when we came out; but we managed to carry notes backwards and forwards, hidden in our shoes or somewhere, which the guards never knew about.

I knew that there was a men's camp up the road; so one day I suggested to Mary Cooper that we should go for a walk in that direction. We found the camp all right and the men were delighted to see us; but when we saw a Japanese car approaching we went on walking as though we didn't know the camp was there. The car passed us and then turned round and came back towards us.

I said to Mary, "We had better turn round and walk back towards the hospital."

The car stopped and two Japanese got out and asked us what we were doing. I replied, "We are hospital nurses; we have been for a walk and now we are going back to the hospital."

They tried to make us get into the car but I refused. However, they insisted on seeing our passes, which they looked at and took away. Eventually, thanks to the good offices of Olga Neubrunner, we did get our passes back, though whether they were the same ones I never discovered. But poor Mary Cooper was so terrified that she vowed she would never go out again.

Whilst we were nursing we had no reason to complain about our treatment as we were left well alone by the Japanese. But at the beginning of March 1943 we were told that we could not visit the POW hospital any more, and when we went out we felt we were being followed. So from that time we only went out when it was absolutely necessary. Soon after this a Japanese doctor took over the hospital and although he was very pleasant to us we did not like him. Discipline was now tightened up and we didn't get nearly so much liberty as before.

On 6 April 1943, we were told to report at the Gunsboe (offices of the Jap civilians) at 12 noon. When we arrived we were kept waiting for two hours and then taken into the office of the Kempei Tai (military police). The only words addressed to us there were, "You blue-eyed English—ugh!"

They spoke to Dr. Holweg for a long time and then started beating him up —also his wife, who went to his assistance. After they had finished their fun they told the doctor, Sister Cooper and myself, to go back to the hospital. We heard that night that the other two had been put into the native jail. Next day the doctor was taken away.

The following morning the Japanese doctor asked us if we would like to continue working in the hospital or go back to camp. Of course we said we would go back to camp. So he said that they would come and fetch us at 1.30 p.m.—which they did—but we did not go to the camp, we stopped at the jail instead. We were searched and then had to wait whilst they turned some natives out of a cell to put us in. Mary and I were in one cell; Olga Neubrunner and Jennie Macalister in another; and the doctor's wife, Mrs Holweg, in another, all on the other side of the jail.

They went into their cells in the white muslin dresses which they had made for themselves. They had no change of clothes, no towel, no soap, no covering of any sort. On the floor was just one rush mat over a stone slab. The cells had one barred window over the door, which was padlocked. After a few days they were each given a sarong in place of their tattered dresses.

Margot continues:

And so began the longest six months of my life. We were allowed out of the cell twice a day for about five minutes. The sanitary arrangements can be left to the imagination. We had two very meagre meals a day and sometimes either cold tea or water. Our fellow prisoners were murderers and thieves, Malayan or Chinese. They were most intrigued to see white women in sarongs. But they were very good to us, as far as they were able, knowing that discovery would mean some form of brutal punishment. When they went out on working parties they would sometimes pass through the bars to us some black coffee in a cigarette tin or maybe a banana or a bit of cake. We never saw the other three, Olga, Jennie or Mrs Holweg, but we were able to get messages to them occasionally via one of the other prisoners. Our cell was large enough for us to walk four paces and that was our exercise. When we went out to wash we collected some stones with which we were able to make chalk marks on the floor and we sometimes played draughts or noughts and crosses with the stones. We got no news of the outside world at all.

After we had been in the cell for two months we were all allowed to walk for half an hour every morning between the two walls of the jail. We had to walk in single file, one metre apart, and we were not allowed to talk. However, after a bit we did manage to say a word or two to the others.

On 10 July (1943) a lot of new people were brought into the jail and the Japanese had to make more room for them. So they moved Mary and me out of our cell and Olga and Jennie out of theirs and put us all four together in a slightly larger one. This was much better for us but it was a very bad day for the rest of the prisoners. Many of those who had been in the jail with us were sent elsewhere and we woke up on the morning of 13 July to find that a lot of new prisoners, many Ambonese men and women and some Dutchmen, had been brought in. Apparently the Kempei Tai had been having a round-up and the jail was full of Japanese guards.

Terrible things then started to happen in the jail; the prisoners were beaten and tortured and many of them died as a result. The things we saw were so horrible that I still can't bear to think—much less talk—about them. We heard afterwards that Dr. Holweg and Dr. Teclecburg were also imprisoned in the jail and were beaten unmercifully. I believe they both died, though I never heard for certain. However, the Japanese appeared to have forgotten our existence.

Olga, who had been in the Malayan Nursing Service before her marriage, started writing poems with a nail on the wall. When she went back to the camp she remembered them and wrote them down for me. Here are some extracts:

The Glimpse of Trees
(through the cell window)

They rise above the roof tops red
The tenderest green against the blue
What constant joy they give to me
As daily I their beauty view.

The ancient ones with mossy limb
And one just like a chestnut tree,
The casuarina's graceful spine
So full of poignant memory.

The Sparrow

He enters our cell with the air of a friend,
Cares not as we walk to and fro.
He knows on our trustiness he can
   depend
And teaches his family so.

141

But when danger threatens or foes cross
  his path
A warrior bold is he;
He fluffs out his feathers and chatters
  with wrath
And away in great terror they flee.

A Prisoner's Thanksgiving

Though weary weeks just come and go
And oft the lamp of hope burns low,
While Freedom's but a word
There's ne'er a day that ends but we
Can raise our hearts in thanks to Thee
For little mercies, Lord.

Jennie became very ill and had all the
symptoms of typhoid fever. Olga, who
could speak a little Malay, badgered the
guards to try to get a doctor—but to no
avail. We knew that in our bag of hoarded
provisions, which had been taken away
from us when we were imprisoned in the
jail, there was a tin of Quaker oats and
some sugar and dried milk. Olga managed
to get permission to go and get it and the
guards let her supervise the making of the
porridge which helped Jennie to turn the

corner and just saved her life—though she was very weak for some time.

Suddenly we were sent for and asked if we would like to stay in jail or go back to the camp. Naturally we opted for the latter—still wondering why we had been put in the jail in the first place. We had had a most ghastly six months but, having seen and heard the atrocities committed on many of our fellow prisoners, we felt lucky to be alive at all.

Margot's own description of this terrible time is simple, if not laconic. But it is not difficult to understand the hardships these four Sisters had withstood. The mental strain of having absolutely nothing to do for six long months, added to the sheer physical misery of their conditions—no soap or water, no change of clothes, most difficult sanitary arrangements, particularly for women, bugs, flies, fleas and all sorts, topped by a climate which is normally only tolerable to Europeans when alleviated by plenty of fresh air, baths, clean clothes, cold drinks and so forth. And on top of all, the strain and anxiety generated by their not knowing *why* they were there—and therefore great uncertainty as to whether they would ever get out. As Olga Neubrunner put it so simply in her poem, "And oft the lamp of hope burns low". The wonder is that it burnt at all.

The Australian Sister, Betty Jeffery, who wrote that wonderful book, *White Coolies*, which was first published in 1954, was in the prison camp with Margot and she wrote to me from her flat at East Malvern, Victoria, Australia, on 2 June 1969, as follows:

I was delighted to read that Dame Margot's story is to be written as she has had a very interesting and unusual career as an Army Nurse starting where we all do and getting to the very top. I am sure QARANC are very proud of her and would want a record of her nursing life with them. Dame Margot is such a fine person, she was liked by all who knew her in that POW camp. I feel her story should be told. I have not done justice to her simply because of the lapse of twenty-seven years since those days and I can't remember the details—only she can do that. I feel that each one of us has a different story to tell.

Margot Turner arrived in the jail at Muntok (Banka Island) with five or six other British Nurses, some days after our arrival there and with the same grim story of their survival at sea. My recollections are hazy now but I do remember these girls looking sunburnt and dreadful when they joined us in Muntok jail—they were blistered, hungry, very thirsty and in a pretty bad way. The Australian Army Nurses had found an old double mattress somewhere and five of us at a time took it in turns to sleep on it, but when we saw these English girls we gave it to them to rest their weary bodies on while they slowly recovered from their ordeal.

They were with us, moving from camp to camp most of the way through the POW years, the exception being one period in 1942 when, fed up with the crowded conditions, they accepted an offer to nurse natives in a clinic in Palembang. We heard on the grapevine later that they were working for two Dutch doctors and had a small place of their own to sleep in at night, and so things at first were a little easier for them.

The next time we saw Margot and the

other English Sisters were early in 1944, when they returned to our camp. We were terribly relieved and pleased to see them. They looked dreadful—their eyes had a wild look in them, they had lost a lot of weight and had been treated very badly by the Japanese. But they were quite sane, even if they didn't look it, though far from well. One of them had to go straight into the camp hospital, where she died some time later. At this time I wrote in *White Coolies*: "What a strong, healthy girl Margot Turner must be! She is a Nursing Sister in Queen Alexandra's Imperial Military Nursing Service, and had already had a shocking time getting from Singapore to Banka Island in February 1942. She was on a raft for five or six days before being picked up by a Japanese destroyer and brought to us at Muntok. Margot was a very sick girl for a long time."

After she recovered Margot was her usual bright self in the camp—we all got on very well together as the British and Australian nurses were always housed near each other.

There was an amusing incident when Margot caught a fowl that flew over the fence. She held it by its legs and kept its beak closed to stop the noise while we discussed whether to be honest and put it back—or kill it and eat it. In fact, from then on we were all doing the same things and sharing the camp nursing and the staffing of the small camp hospital, calling ourselves "District Nurses" and the others "hospital staff". This was a full-time job until the end as there were more sick people than healthy people over the last year or so there.

Margot was always a very happy, pleasant, easy to talk to person and she had a lot of fun in her; and if there was anything doing, Margot was in it up to the neck—she was a popular person in the camp and liked by all there who knew her. It was quite a sad day when, after we were released, we had to say goodbye and go our separate ways.

I saw Margot when I was in London in 1950–52 and we never miss corresponding with each other at Christmas. We will always be good friends.

So Margot recovered from her period in prison; but there is no doubt that the six months of close confinement was a great strain on the four nurses and it was probably largely as a result of it that Olga Neubrunner died in the camp on 22 March 1945 and Mary Cooper on 26 June of the same year.

After the war, Major P. R. H. Turner, Margot's brother, was determined to see if he could discover the reason why Margot and her other three companions should suddenly, without any reason given, be confined in a cell in the jail which housed Malays and Chinese on capital charges. But the Japanese were adepts at covering up on this sort of barbaric behaviour—of which there were so many examples. They went through all the motions of leaving no stone unturned to uncover the matter and eventually produced the following bit of flannel from the Staff Officer of the 25th Japanese Army Headquarters at Padang, dated 18 December 1945.

British Nurse E. M. Turner

We have been ordered by HQ 25th Army to investigate the reasons why the above-named person was interned in a prison for six months from April 1943. We have tried to find the truth of the reasons why the above-named person was interned in prison during the said period but because of the lack of papers referring to and also being unable to locate the exact persons concerned in this incident we regret that we are unable to produce fuller reports.

Nevertheless we report herewith an incident similar to the one asked.

Dutch Medical doctor and wife—Hall Waige (spelling uncertain—translator)

Nurses—(Names unknown)

The above named having professional standings as a Doctor and Nurses were, by their wishes and under pledge (whether all of them dually [*sic*] sweared or not is uncertain) released from confinement in the early part of 1943 to serve on the staff of the Palembang Residency Hospital.

In April 1943 at the time of anti-air drill, they did nothing whatever to heed the orders to darken the lights of the hospital though warned to several times. Therefore Mr. Waige and wife who were in charge of the hospital were called in for questioning. They were not only unable to explain the reasons of not carrying out the orders but displayed antagonistic emotions and furthermore showed no signs of wishing to co-operate with the Civil Administration. Summarizing along with their daily activities, they were charged with the suspicion of communicating with the enemy as well as breaking the rules and regulations of a released Hostile National and forthwith interned for further investigation.

The local prison under the supervision of the Civil Police being for natives, it was seen both unwise and unfit to have them interned along with the natives where the sanitary conditions were bad. Therefore they were placed in another internment house under Japanese control. They were not treated as ordinary prisoners and given many privileges, such as the receiving of food from without and the possession of anything they wished.

The other nurses upon the internment of the doctor and his wife refused to remain at their post at the hospital and asked that they should be returned to the Internment Camp. They were like the others, under suspect of also communicating with the enemy and, as a means of preventing espionage, were interned along with the others.

After carrying out various investigations no definite evidence could be found to confirm the charge of the above-stated suspicion and also of their change of attitude were released and sent to the Internment Camp in September of the same year.

Peter Turner made some rather rude marginal notes to this diatribe which I have not included above.

7

Back to Internment

TO continue Margot's story in her own words:

The 22nd September 1943—and our first glimpse of freedom after six months in jail. It was nearly a year since we had left the camp and all our friends and we were eager to hear what had been happening to them. We found the camp had just been moved and we were now living where the men had been, in wooden huts, shut off completely from the outside world. As usual the Japs had been as unhelpful as possible over the move, of which our people had been given very short notice. Only three or four native trucks had been allowed to move five hundred women and childen—and all their possessions. Those who couldn't walk just had to ride with the baggage as best they could.

The new camp had been constructed on swampy ground below sea level and it was thick with bugs, rats, fleas and mosquitoes. As the men prisoners, who had previously been occupying it, thought that the Japs were taking it over for their own use, they had deliberately left it in a filthy condition and the women had to work very hard to get it into a habitable state. The whole area of the camp was only about a hundred yards long by forty yards wide and into this confined space five hundred people had to be crammed. The actual space allowed per person was twenty-seven inches and in it we each had to keep our few personal belongings. Sixty people were crammed into each hut, which meant that we had to sleep on a narrow mat, side by side like sardines in a tin. The huts had been built along three sides of the rectangular shaped area, with a Guard house at the camp entrance, on one side of which was the little camp hospital of about twenty beds. The hut opposite the hospital was occupied by fifty Dutch nuns who ran the hospital under the doctor in charge, a rather unpleasant German Jewess.

At one end of the camp both British and Dutch kitchens were established side by side. The two bathrooms for the entire camp consisted of cement troughs designed for the storage of water. The lavatories were nothing more than cement drains extending off from the bathrooms. The Japanese had refused to allow the services of coolies to clean and empty these primitive latrines and the women prisoners had to do it themselves—and indeed, all the other daily manual labour required in the camp.

The huts were found to be not only filthy but vermin-infested; and for the latter condition the Japanese refused to provide any insecticide. The roofs of the huts, made of attap, or thatch, were not rainproof and the women and children often had to sleep on wet boards.

We experienced at once a great hardship in not having the men's camp close to us in that the daily trucks of firewood ceased to arrive and we had to chop wood ourselves every day, with a very blunt axe, to provide fuel for cooking.

We were all living at such close quarters

and under such trying conditions that our tempers occasionally got a bit frayed. But even so the Japs couldn't get us down. They hated the British and if anything was wrong it was always the bad British who had caused the trouble. They simply couldn't understand why we went about smiling and singing. They told us we ought to be serious as there was a war on. One thing I was always thankful for was my sense of humour; it was just as well that the Japs didn't realize how much we laughed at them.

Naturally, when we got back to the camp, all our friends were anxious to hear about our experiences in jail; and we of course were eager to know what had been going on in our absence. They had managed to have quite a good Christmas in the previous camp. The British and Dutch in the men's camp had sent them some supplies and, most welcome of all things, some soap! The men had also sent a huge piece of beef and some vegetables—so the women had been able to have a festive Christmas dinner. And they had also celebrated the New Year—again with the help of some meat and vegetables from the men's camp. More and more women continued to arrive in the camp, some of them Malays, lousy with scabies and fleas.

One of the greatest hardships was the lack of water. The Japs had cut off the pipe supply and the internees had to go out in the heat of the day and draw their ration of water. They then had to carry it back up a steep hill to the camp. The Japs had also become much more strict about "Tenko", which they had got into the habit of having every day. Clothes were in shorter and shorter supply—and consequently briefer! Nevertheless we had continued to try to look as respectable as we could.

One of the good things that had happened was the establishment of a regular ambulance service which conveyed the sick to the general hospital in Palembang. As the sick men from near-by camps were treated in the same hospital it became a channel of underground communication, of which both the men and women made the fullest use. But it had to be done with the greatest care—or the most severe punishment would descend upon them. The male internees in the vicinity were given small money payments by the Japs for work on which they were engaged and they very generously made small payments to the women in our camp who were sick or without any funds—which allowed them to buy additions to the meagre diet. The Japs made a distinction between male internees and captured prisoners of war, to the considerable detriment of the latter who were as badly, if not worse, off than we were with regard to rations and other amenities. The lorries delivering supplies made their first call at the male internee camp so it was not too difficult for them to slip in some extra items of diet for the women's camp. They also sometimes managed to pass along items of news which they had obtained from their secret radio; but this very soon got too dangerous as discovery would have involved them, and probably the women too, in terrible punishment. However, all these things stopped when the move to the new camp took place in September 1943.

Christmas 1943 was much quieter than the previous one as there were no men to provide us with a Christmas dinner; but we managed to concoct something special —and the camp vocal choir and orchestra functioned better than ever. Norah Chambers, who had a good voice herself, had gathered around her an "orchestra" which sang and—in the absence of any musical instruments—hummed the music written from memory by Miss Dryburgh. The effect of an orchestra was created by humming the four parts of soprano, second soprano, contralto and second contralto, representing the four stringed instruments, that is violin, viola, cello and double bass. The music was the most wonderful thing in our lives and I don't know what we should have done without it.

Ruth Russell-Roberts also became a keen member of this choir, which consisted of thirty women of different nationalities.

To continue Margot's story:

In February 1944 we were allowed to have another daily shop, brought in by the Chinese. The range of commodities was somewhat limited—mostly bananas, a few eggs, dry biscuits, onions and soya beans. And most of us tried to do some job which would bring us in the wherewithal to buy these little luxuries. Food was now beginning to get less—not so much rice and fewer vegetables; but we did occasionally get fresh fish and what fun we used to have killing and scaling them without any proper knives.

One day a cockerel strayed into the camp. It had obviously come from one of the near-by Japanese houses. There was one mad rush to see who could catch it. The poor creature was terrified and made rather a lot of noise. We were afraid the guard would hear and wonder what was happening. After a great struggle I eventually caught it, and it was killed, plucked and in the pot in a matter of minutes. Again we hoped that the guard would not do a round and look in the cooking pot, as he often did. Luck was with us, and that evening about sixteen people had a very small taste of chicken. We often wondered whether the Japs had missed their cockerel. Most of our cooking was done in old tins, and it was a sad day for us if any of them sprang a leak.

I was now in charge of the wood squad,

a very important and strenuous assignment. It meant that at any time of the day we would have to carry in huge logs, which first had to be divided between the Dutch and British kitchens, as did all the rations which came into the camp. We also had to carry in the sacks of rice from a shed outside the camp where it was stored. Some of the sacks were only half full or had holes in them and we stuffed into our pockets any precious bits of rice which fell to the ground. The cutting up of the logs was a most awful chore.

Sometimes some very odd things came in for the rations. Margot describes how one day the Japs brought in a dead monkey as the meat ration for over six hundred people. Her comment—"it made a very tasty stew". Whenever they got a banana they would cook the skins and eat them.

When human beings are thrown together in desperate and hopeless circumstances such as these, it usually happens that the crisis produces its own personalities and leaders. Certainly this women's camp of six hundred people, of different races, creeds and languages, would have been in a much worse way if this had not happened. There had to be some acceptance of discipline if the camp was not to disintegrate into what, in happier political times, might have been termed inflation—or too much money chasing too few goods. Here it was a case of too much hunger chasing too few rations; too much sickness for too few medicines; too much despair chasing too little hope.

Margot recalls:

Two outstanding people had been chosen as the Camp Commandants of the British Internees and of the Dutch. The former was a Mrs Hinch, who had been a passenger from Singapore on the *Giang Bee*, which had been sunk in the Banka Strait. She was an American by birth but married to an Englishman and had spent the last twenty years in Malaya, where her husband had been the Principal of an Anglo-Chinese Methodist School in Singapore. He had been interned in the Civilian Camp in Changi. Mrs Hinch was a woman of placid temperament and quiet dignity who was never afraid to stand up to the Japs on any matter which seemed capable of adjustment. The Dutch Commandant, the Rev. Mother Laurentia, was another fine character, with great common sense and the ability to tackle the many difficulties which arose.

By this time the money in the camp was becoming exhausted and it was more difficult to buy the little extras in the black market. Now it was jewellery which was being exchanged for cash and many sentimental and treasured ornaments had to be exchanged for very little money. Ruth Russell-Roberts had a pair of earrings which Denis had given her on their marriage, an engagement ring, a bracelet, a diamond wrist watch and a three-banded emerald and diamond eternity ring. One by one they found their way over the wire until only the eternity ring remained. This she was determined to keep at all costs. It was extraordinary really that the Japs had allowed the internees to keep such jewellery.

Ruth had been much saddened by the death of her friend Valda Godley, who had never been able to digest the rice and therefore got weaker and weaker. Without any medicine or change of food it had been impossible to save her.

Margot continues her story:

On 1 April 1944, the administration of the camp had been transferred from civil to military control and from then on life became more and more difficult for the prisoners. Everything had to be done with military precision under the orders of Captain Siki, the new Camp Commandant. First of all we had to be gathered in national groups and "presented" one by one, being made to bow obsequiously as our names were read out. Even the babies had to be presented. Everyone had to give their personal particulars and their ages and were to be weighed every month—presumably to see how much work we had left in us.

Siki gathered us all together and made a long speech which was relayed to us by an interpreter. The news of the war was of course devoted to a build-up of the great and all-conquering Japanese Empire. But he did say one thing which suggested that they might not be so all-powerful after all. There was a danger, he said, of air raids and in such an eventuality we must be prepared to evacuate at short notice to a near-by rubber estate. Giving this as an excuse the concerts were stopped and, in fact, anything which gave us a little pleasure. The rations were cut and gradually became less and less; but they did come in regularly and in some cases were of better quality, particularly the rice; some sugar and salt were provided and the vegetable ration, though cut by half, was quite filling. Half a cup of tea per person per month was issued and a kerosine tin of red palm-oil arrived—not much for six hundred people. But the lack of soap was a great hardship; the only means of washing was to stand out in the rain.

On the credit side, however, the new jailers gave us all a preventive injection against typhoid, dysentery and cholera. This was a life-saver to many. But the worst and most debilitating innovation was the amount of heavy manual labour we were forced to undertake. Working parties had to be organized to unload the rations, which were brought in to the camp in military lorries. The sacks of rice, which formed the greater part of the supplies, would have taxed our strength severely even if we had been in good physical condition; but in our debilitated state the work of moving the sacks left us utterly exhausted.

Siki then announced that, as the food situation in Sumatra was becoming acute, the prisoners would be required to cultivate gardens within the camp for their vegetable supply. The area we had to dig was the space in the centre of the camp, consisting of hard clay, and also some ground outside the camp. All the digging had to be done with heavy hoes which made little impression on the iron-hard ground and jarred the diggers horribly at every stroke. In addition we had to tidy up the roads outside the camp, including the gardens of the houses in which the Japs were living, and clean their drains daily.

The water supply in this camp was very poor and often we only had one small tin of water in which to wash ourselves *and* our clothes; and the drinking water was very limited indeed. It is not difficult to imagine the hardship imposed by this lack of water; after all the filthy and dirty jobs we were forced to do we virtually never got clean. Some of the prisoners were allowed to go, in the heat of the afternoon, to fetch buckets of water from a hydrant about half a mile down the road. But first they had to fill the baths of the Japanese houses, and then water the gardens in the camp, which were hard and dry as a bone. This water fatigue meant several trips to the hydrant, but after all their labour they would be lucky to get one bucket of drinking water into the camp.

All this heavy manual work went on—in a tropical climate—every day from 5 a.m. to 6 p.m., with a break of three hours in the middle of the day. The British prisoners protested strongly that many of our members were quite unfit to undertake this arduous labour, but all our protests were unavailing. This, more than any other single factor, accounted for the many deaths of prisoners in the following months.

During the month of April there was great excitement in the camp when a party of British women arrived to add to their numbers. These were the first British newcomers the prisoners had seen since their internment. One of the newcomers had been the Matron of a British General Hospital; there were several British Sisters, a Scottish doctor, a civilian nurse (Miss Netta Smith), three Dutch women and a few Eurasians. They now had four women doctors in the camp, whose services were much in demand.

Margot Turner soon made the acquaintance of Netta Smith, with whom she struck up a close and lasting friendship. Netta Smith, a small, sturdy Scot from Aberdeen, possessed of an indomitable spirit, was a civilian nurse who had been evacuated from Singapore in the *Kuala* on 13 February 1942. She had lost all her possessions in the bombing and boarded the ship in her white uniform, white stockings and white shoes—without even a handbag.

Netta had sat on the deck, looking at the blazing inferno of Singapore with great sorrow as she knew and loved the Island so well. One of her friends, Sister MacFarlane, had been killed by a bomb splinter sitting beside her on the deck of the *Kuala* before the ship had even weighed anchor; and a Eurasian girl who was with her was also killed. On the ship with them were a number of wounded men, including a Naval officer who had been on board HMS *Repulse*; he had been one of her patients on the Island in the Johore Bahru Hospital. Netta was with him and the other wounded when the *Kuala* was sunk next day. She describes the casualties from the bombing of the ship as "terrible".

Netta Smith had no lifejacket and the gangway to the upper deck was packed with Chinese, who were petrified with fear and uncertain whether to stay on the ship or trust themselves to the water. Her wounded officer from the *Repulse* was already swimming away from the sinking ship. Dead bodies were lying all over the deck and floating in the water. Netta grasped a rope that was hanging down over the side and lowered herself into the sea. Many people were swimming around. Netta was not a very strong swimmer but was confident she could keep herself afloat. And when the Japanese bombers came over again and began machine-gunning the people in the water she dived down each time—as Margot Turner had done.

Eventually Netta saw a wooden box floating in the water and she encouraged a small Eurasian girl to hang on to it with her. They were then both picked up by a ship's boat, which had come from the island to help. The boat was being rowed by a Mr. Ross of the Malayan Public Works Department, and a young British soldier, Private Fraser. They also picked up Dr. Margaret Thompson, a married woman who had been living in Singapore with her husband. After a time the boat was packed with people, many hanging on to the sides. Some of the people in the boat were dead and these they put overboard. They fetched up at last on a very small, uninhabited island, where there were already about forty survivors—ten Europeans and the remainder Chinese and Eurasian. It was bitterly cold at night and they lay huddled close together to keep warm. There they stayed for three days and three nights with nothing to eat or drink. Once a sea bird flew overhead with a large fish in its mouth. They created such a hullabaloo that the poor bird dropped the fish —which they divided into small pieces and ate raw. They had several wounded people with them and all they could do to help them was to bathe their wounds in sea water.

Suddenly Mr. Ross spotted a small Chinese sailing junk that traded between the islands with coconut husks and dried fish. He rowed out to the junk in his small boat and asked if they would take the party on board. The Chinese, however, stipulated that they must be paid 300 dollars. Most of the party had no money at all; but they had a whip-round and one Chinese woman, with four children, produced practically the whole sum herself. The crew of the junk gave them each some rice, some salt fish and a little water. The junk was crawling with beetles but no one complained—they were saved, anyway for the time being.

When they arrived at their destination, however, another and bigger island, the Malays were very hostile. They said that there were Japanese all round and the escapees must leave at once. But the Chinese took them in and fed them—even producing a tot of whisky each—which cheered them up a lot. As soon as it was dark the Chinese took them off in a small sailing ship.

Having arrived at another little island they found several more Europeans and Netta met a friend, Sarah Service (later Mrs. Beeton), who had been with her in the Johore Bahru Hospital. They established a small hospital on this island, treated those who were sick or wounded, and sent them over in junks to the larger Dutch island of Sinkep, where there was a Dutch tin mine with quite a sizeable hospital attached to it.

This was a lovely island and the patients were nursed there for several weeks and, as they became convalescent, were sent over in small batches to Sumatra. Quite a lot of these patients picked up ships on the far side of Sumatra and got away to Ceylon—and even to Australia.

Luck played an extraordinary part in deciding human fate in these waters at this particular stage of the war. Some people would arrive on one island, be picked up by some rickety old boat and get clean away from the Japs; others would appear to be in clover and suddenly find themselves landed in prison. A number of those who passed through the hands of Netta Smith and her fellow nurses at this time got a passage to safety. Netta herself hadn't seen or heard of a Jap since she escaped from the *Kuala*. But it was then decided that they should follow their patients to Sumatra. Their ship, however, broke down and they had to return to Sinkep—and suddenly, along came the Japs and rounded them all up.

Their party now amounted to about thirty —of different nationalities. They were taken up the Djambi river and imprisoned in Djambi jail; and there they remained until

April 1944. Towards the end of this time, however, they left the jail and were interned in a school with a large number of Dutch women. Netta says, "The Djambi doctor was extremely nice to us, as were several of the officers, but the other ranks were pretty brutal at times and Dr. Thompson was very badly treated on her way out to see a patient. We had to put up with a good deal of real hunger too."

They were then moved to Palembang, where Netta met up with Margot Turner and also with an old friend, Jennie Macalister. By this time some of the women in Netta Smith's party had very little clothing left. She says, "The Folies Bergères weren't in it. My one suit of white uniform had fallen to pieces and I had a tiny pair of briefs and a small bra— and several others were in like case."

Netta goes on to describe Margot:

... She had a very strong personality and if anything important had to be done she was always there to do it. We did a lot together in the latter part of our captivity. Fortunately I kept remarkably fit and was never in hospital. I had injections from the doctor in Djambi for malaria and dysentery but still had bouts of malaria all through the last camps. . . .

Margot and I got on well with the Australian Sisters, who sat at a bench alongside us for their meals. They were very good and worked very hard but a number of them never came through. Margot and I were the poorest of the poor and were determined to make some money. Others had kept a certain amount of money with them and some had bits of jewellery with which they could get extras. So we took on the worst job in the camp—looking after the latrines—and the others were only too glad to pay us to do it. It most certainly had to be done —by someone. The latrines were quite awful—just huge, long drains, with wooden planks for seats; and the drains were full of maggots. Margot and I were paid ten dollars a week each for this filthy job—and my word we earned it!

To add to their other discomforts they had a plague of rats and spiders, which were particularly frightening to the children—and not too pleasant for the grown-ups either.

The following poem was written by a fellow prisoner who died during captivity, and demonstrates clearly the affection and admiration that people had for Margot:

To Margot
(On her birthday 10 May 1944)

With eyes that are blue as a mountain
pool
Reflecting the sky in its fastness cool,
With limbs straight and strong and a nut
brown skin,
There's joy for the eye just to see you
come in.

Yet every call for a volunteer band
Will find you first there with your willing
hand.
No matter the task whatsoever it be,
Your curly head there I'll be sure to see.

You are hauling great logs 'neath the
noon-day sun
And hungry and tired, but the job must
be done,
Chopping and cooking and chunkelling
too,
No task too unpleasant, no toilers too
few.

Your calmness and courage and enduring
  power
Have carried you through life's bitterest
  hour,
So may the good Lord bless your
  birthday today,
And fill you with joy as you go on your
  way.

The Japs continued their monthly
weighings, which told them that the women
continued to lose weight and few were over
seven stone. Not that the Japs did anything
about it except that, towards the end of May,
they paid the prisoners a small sum,
amounting to eight shillings a month, which
came in useful and enabled some small luxuries to be purchased. In July Commandant
Siki again addressed the prisoners and told
them they must expect some bombs—but
he would die with them in the rubble. This
cheered them up a lot! He again warned that
food would get less and that the prisoners
must work more and not sing so much. The
irksome "Tenko" was now fixed for 1 p.m.,
the hottest hour of the day when even the
natives slept. Altogether their lot was not a
happy one.

The 11th of August 1944 was the most thrilling day the British prisoners had had since their captivity began. Just after dark, as they were settling down for the night, they heard the sound of aircraft and the crump of falling bombs, followed by the immediate stutter of ack-ack fire from the guns protecting the big oil refinery at Pladjou. The town's sirens screamed and the Japs went mad. All the lights went out in the camp area and all hell was let loose. It was just like Singapore three years earlier. The British and Australian prisoners were hopping with excitement as waves of planes kept coming over until almost daylight. All the boasting of the Japanese that the British and Americans had been sunk without trace was shown to be lies, lies, lies.

Next morning the Japs in the camp tried to make out that it was an anti-aircraft practice; but the prisoners knew what falling bombs sounded like from bitter experience.

By this time the British were working a system of community cooking. This provided a small bowl of rice and water porridge at 7 a.m.; black coffee at 10 a.m.; at mid-day a small bowl of rice with a dessertspoon of vegetables and some highly flavoured seasoning known as sambal, which was very popular; and in the evening another bowl of rice with some vegetable, after which they sat around talking in groups, drinking coffee made from the grounds of the morning coffee. Their one great joy lay in the wonderful sunsets.

The prisoners were now more crowded in the camp than ever and water got scarcer and scarcer. The mothers of small children, of whom there were quite a number, had a terrible time trying to get enough water to wash their offspring *and* their clothes. The water shortage was one of the greatest cruelties inflicted by the Japs and one which they refused to do anything to alleviate.

Most of the Australian and British prisoners were now trying to earn their living—the have-nots giving service to the haves. They made clothes from the rush bags in which the fish came, patched shorts and made sun hats. Some went over to the Dutch lines to do various domestic chores for them—such as laundry, cleaning out their rooms and taking their children out. Others made slippers and sandals from odd bits of material, and still others cut hair with nail scissors, carried water for the Dutch prisoners at so much a bucket, chopped wood, pounded soya beans, and made rag dolls for their children. All these chores, on top of the very heavy manual work they were compelled to do, took a lot out of them—but every penny earned meant a banana, or perhaps a banana skin, and food meant life.

The concerts were now allowed to start up again on a limited scale and some special comic shows were put on for the children. The 17th of August 1944 was another great milestone in the dreary existence of the prisoners, when the first batch of letters arrived from the outside world—the first they had ever received. There was of course disappointment for many who didn't get a letter, and heartbreak for some whose letter contained bad news. Mrs. Hinch and a Dutchwoman, Mrs. Muller, who spoke Japanese, had to sign for every letter with the Jap officers watching.

It was a wonderful moment for Betty Jeffrey when she suddenly saw a letter from Australia addressed in her mother's hand. It only consisted of twenty-five words. But temporarily the whole of the misery of camp life was wiped out and she was living in another world. Ruth Russell-Roberts, after two and a half years of anxiety, heard of her daughter Lynette's safe arrival in London. She had hoped against hope all those months, but in view of the many sinkings of ships which had left Singapore at that time, she knew that the odds were against it.

Margot was one of the unlucky ones who got no letter. In fact she didn't receive one at all until July 1945, just before the prisoners were told that the war was over. It must have been a bitter moment for the unlucky ones; but the fact that some letters had been delivered to the camp meant that someone from the outside world did know of their existence. And this was a comforting thought. The prisoners were then allowed to write a brief postcard; but Margot's never arrived and she never expected it to leave the camp.

On the same day that the letters came a British plane dived over the town of Palembang before climbing up again into the clouds and the prisoners hoped that it was meant to signify that the presence of their camp was known.

Margot recalls:

179

A few days later some American Red Cross boxes arrived, some of them pilfered, but others intact. The boxes were unpacked by the Japanese camp policemen—whom the Japs called "Heyhoes"—amidst great excitement. The contents were handed over to the Canteen Committee and shared equally. Each prisoner received twenty-two cigarettes, one inch of chocolate, four lumps of sugar and a spoonful of butter; and a half pound tin of jam had to be shared between fourteen people. However, it was better than nothing—and what with the letters and parcels our spirits rose.

But these good happenings were soon followed by news which dashed all our spirits to zero. Siki announced that we were to be moved back to Muntok on Banka Island—where apparently the civilian male internees had been sent when they left Palembang. It was not that we were sorry to leave the sordid camp at Palembang, but we felt that the Japs would not be sending us to Muntok unless they thought that the end of the war was still a long way off. Also, and much worse, the journey would be a terrible ordeal for

180

people in our condition and, quite apart from the deaths which were bound to take place during the journey, many more would inevitably result from the hardships entailed.

On 21 and 30 August we were all given injections—presumably against typhoid —but we were not told what the injections were for and they made us all feel sick and depressed. We had no idea when the move was to take place; but, in the meanwhile, there were air alerts almost every night, with the Japs running to and fro, in and out of the air raid shelters. The war was getting a bit closer and the Japs were intent on hiding us.

If only the prisoners could have known that, nearly three months earlier, the British and American liberation forces had landed in Normandy and were thrusting forward towards Germany in co-operation with the Russians advancing from the east, they would have been given the strength and the "will to live".

Margot relates how the Japanese appeared to be scared to death of the air raids. "At first," she says, "they began to give out some extra food; but, on 30 September, the rice ration was again cut and the small fish ration stopped altogether. When we complained the rice sacks, which were always weighed before issue, were found to contain a lot of stones."

Towards the end of September some more American Red Cross parcels arrived, which were openly pilfered and enjoyed by the Japanese and Hey-hoe guards. However, early in October, part of a consignment of Red Cross parcels was distributed to the prisoners and this gave a small but wonderful little ration to each one. But this was a very small proportion of the whole because so much had already been stolen by the guards.

8

Muntok Once More

SUDDENLY, early in October, the prisoners were told that the dreaded move to Muntok was about to start. Margot describes it as follows:

We went in groups over a period of about ten days. The Australian Sisters were in the first contingent and we were in the last. I gathered that their journey was no picnic but ours was certainly one of unspeakable hardship and discomfort. First we were packed into open trucks, having had to load all our own possessions and a lot belonging to the Japanese; then we transferred into a three-decker river boat where we were herded together like a lot of cattle. It was appallingly hot and we got very little food or drink.

Late the next afternoon we anchored off Muntok pier, down which I had been carried by the Japanese doctor when I was

183

first put ashore from the battleship two and a half years earlier. It seemed a lifetime ago. Then we had that awful walk along the pier carrying our possessions, during which several of the women fainted from sheer exhaustion. From there we continued the journey in open trucks.

When we eventually arrived at the camp the Australians were very good to us, they had food ready for us and looked after us in a most wonderful way. The men, who were now located in the old coolie camp which we had first inhabited, had been equally good to them when they had first arrived and had given them food and gallons of tea. As soon as we had had something to eat and drink we fell into an exhausted sleep. This was by far our worst move, partly I suppose because we were that much weaker.

The new camp was a vast improvement on the verminous squalor of Palembang. It was huge, brand new and spotlessly clean. It was situated high enough above sea level for us to enjoy the sea air and the attap huts allowed plenty of bed space; each person had a new rush mat on which to sleep. It was built on a gravel surface and the six big huts—somewhat jerry-built and tied, rather than nailed, together—were each capable of housing a hundred and forty people. There were three huge kitchens, one main kitchen in the middle of the camp and the other two, containing about fifty small concrete fire-places each, were two huts away from the main kitchen. Unfortunately, the lat-rines, which consisted of cement pits, were right alongside the kitchens. The community bathrooms, cement-floored and boarded up with attap only, were next door to the latrines. The camp possessed nine wells, cemented and clean, but the water soon ran out. All the wells were empty within twenty-four hours, which meant fetching water from a tiny creek about ten minutes' walking distance from the camp.

Although arduous this water fatigue had its attractions as the creek was situated beyond a stretch of jungle country in which a number of wild flowers grew, while the creek itself offered opportunities for a bathe and a wash such as we had not experienced for years.

But the prisoners soon discovered that life in the new camp was not all jam; in fact it turned out to be as near hell as makes no matter. Much of our luggage had been rifled and precious valuables and small hoards of food had been stolen. There was much hard manual labour to be done in erecting a barbed-wire fence round the hospital and the sinking of heavy posts. Because of the great shortage of food which became worse as every month went by, we were forced to work long hours in the gardens. Every day we had to go out of the camp with chunkals to help grow sweet potatoes over an ever-increasing acreage. The Dutch and the British worked in separate but adjoining plots. There was one consolation, however; the wood situation was easier.

But all the time we were getting weaker and our numbers fewer. The days in Muntok were hot and humid and the nights were cold. Three years of hard labour on a starvation diet had already taken a heavy toll of more than fifty lives. There were many cases of malaria, beri-beri and dysentery—with no medicines to deal with them. And now a new fever fell upon the camp; it occurred suddenly and produced raging temperatures and unconsciousness, followed by skin irritation. For want of a better name we called it "Banka Fever". My theory was that it originated from the creek, from which we obtained all our water.

Fortunately, the camp hospital was much bigger and better organized than that in Palembang. There was a ward which could take nineteen patients, and a children's ward. In addition there was an infectious block consisting of four small rooms, taking three patients in each. Fifty yards away was a convalescent hospital which was bigger and more airy; this took about thirty patients. But there were now over seven hundred people in the camp, most of the newcomers being Eurasians. The four doctors—all women—in the camp, and a team of Australian and British nurses, were kept continually on duty. And in view of the emergency the trained Nursing Sisters were relieved of their camp chores in order to be able to give more time to nursing—which of course was what we had always wanted to do.

The Dutch nuns, who had formerly worked as nurses in Charitas Hospital in Palembang, continued to staff the hospital and they worked heroically. One of them did all the laundry for the whole hospital, and the sick, in an oil drum. Another spent her entire time cooking for the sick and making hot drinks for the chronically ill. Like the nurses in the hospitals in the last days of Singapore these nuns behaved like angels and the British and Australian Sisters were full of admiration for these heroic women.

Of the four doctors, one looked after the hospital, another was in charge of convalescents and the daily clinic, whilst the other two were flat out looking after the six blocks in the camp.

The British and Australian Sisters got together and decided to divide into two main groups, hospital staff and district nurses. This was the only way to cope with the dreadful Banka fever, which had hit the camp and continued to recur every few weeks. The Dutch civilian nurses stopped nursing, with one exception, although there were many trained nurses amongst the five hundred Dutch internees. Sister Reynolds, a nun, and the Australian Sister, Jean Ashton, acted as joint Matrons in the hospital. All the Japanese did to help in this emergency was to bring in a small bottle of one hundred quinine tablets for seven hundred people once every six weeks—which was practically useless.

Night duty was a nightmare for the Sisters, with only one oil lamp and plenty of pitfalls to fall into.

During the last part of November conditions continued to get worse and at one time there were well over two hundred people down with Banka fever, many of them British. There had been no contact with the men's jail and it was thought perhaps they were getting the epidemic there as well. Naturally the death rate rose rapidly—particularly amongst mothers with children who had often starved themselves to keep the children alive. We had to dig the graves, construct rough coffins and conduct the burials. The dead were carried to a small Chinese cemetery in the jungle where a special corner had been marked out for the camp. Digging the graves would have been easier if we had had any spades; the chunkals provided made this task long and heavy. Either the nuns or the missionaries took the burial services at the gravesides. The cemetery was in a very pretty spot on the hillside among a profusion of wild flowers. The two Commandants, Mother Laurentia and Mrs. Hinch, insisted that the Japanese should provide small wooden crosses to mark the graves and inscriptions were burnt on these by Norah Chambers and Mrs. Owen.

In the last week of November the Japs produced some money which had been sent by the American Red Cross. This was a great help; but black market prices were rising so rapidly that the money was soon spent. The third Christmas in prison camp came and went without very much attempt at any celebrations.

Margot Turner and Netta Smith, both incredibly tough in body and spirit, were a great source of strength to one another— and indeed to all around them. Netta remarks:

Some people who had so much to live for, married women with husbands interned, and children at school, just gave up and said they could not go on living indefinitely in this fashion. I suppose I was one of those hardy Scots; I was determined to get out of the camp come what may. The Japs expected you to bow and curtsy. I avoided them when I could but if I couldn't, then I bowed and curtsied and I was never knocked about as some of the others were. They tried to humiliate us in any way they could—tried to get us down and knock the cockiness out of us. One Australian girl was made to stand for hours in the blazing sun for something she had done—and she died. I managed to keep out of any scrapes. But then I'm a canny Scot—a true Aberdonian!

Both Margot and Netta had one great asset—their sense of humour. It enabled them to keep things in some sort of perspective. They were both reasonable women who had learnt to control their emotions. In spite of their terrible plight things couldn't go on like this for ever. Either the British or the Japanese would win the war some day and then there would be peace—if they could only hold on. But as they entered the New Year of 1945 many women were running out of strength, running out of hope, running out of life itself. Like courage, morale and hope are expendable; people only have so much of these qualities —though some have more than others. There is a lot of luck about dying, just as there is about living. If a person had a bad go of Banka fever the chances were they wouldn't recover—however strong their physique and however high their morale. Truly "Hope deferred maketh the heart sick". If only they could have known how long their ordeal was likely to last.

By January 1945 seventy-seven bodies had been carried out to the little Chinese cemetery. Ruth Russell-Roberts and Christine Bundy had both gone down with Banka fever together and lay in hospital side by side. Christine recovered and was able to return to her hut but Ruth lay in the throes of the dreaded fever, weak and helpless.

At the beginning of October 1944 Denis Russell-Roberts, on a working party on an airfield in Singapore, made the acquaintance of a Sergeant in the Japanese Air Force who knew a little English and was a more friendly and better educated type than his fellows. He was also quite keen to improve his English and he and Denis got talking. In the course of conversation he said he would shortly be flying to Palembang in Sumatra. At last Denis had met someone whom he felt might help him get a letter to Ruth. He worked on the Sergeant gradually, got him to show a photo of his wife, and then told him about Ruth and Lynette. Finally he asked the man if he would take a letter to Ruth. At first the Sergeant refused to have anything to do with it; it would be much too dangerous and the Kempei Tai might search his kit. Denis wisely did not press the matter; but two days later the man said he would take the letter.

So Denis typed a long letter all about their camp, and Lynette, and their coming reunion, which he felt could not now be long delayed. The secret camp wireless indicated that the war would soon be over—information which the women's camp at Muntok would have dearly loved to know. He was careful not to mention anything which might compromise his Sergeant friend if the letter was found on him. It was a letter full of love and hope. Denis only told a few of his friends about it and they all thought he was very foolish to trust this man. But Denis felt he had to take the chance. And so, in due course, the Japanese Sergeant flew off to Palembang with the letter. How could Denis know that Ruth was now at Muntok?

As Ruth got weaker she agreed to sell her three-banded eternity ring, the only thing she had left that Denis had given her. There was a pretty little Indonesian girl of twenty in the camp, called Julia Roos, who worked for a Dutch woman running a black market racket with the natives beyond the wire. On 18 January it was arranged that a Hey-hoe would send to the camp some food and money in exchange for this lovely ring and that Julia would meet him at a rendezvous outside the wire.

The first night Julia narrowly escaped being raped by one of the Japanese guards. But she bravely tried again the following night, taking another Indonesian girl with her. Before they got to the rendezvous, however, they were accosted by another man who spoke to Julia in the Muntok language and handed her a letter for "a lady in the camp". He then took to his heels and ran. Placing the letter in the pocket of her jacket Julia and her companion sat down to wait the arrival of the native who was due to bring the expected foodstuffs. By ten o'clock the girls were back in camp and both food and letter were handed over to the Dutch woman.

Later that night Christine read Denis's letter to Ruth. She simply nodded and smiled, turned over on her left side and fell into a deep sleep.

The next day the English Sisters buried her in the little cemetery among the jungle flowers and marked her grave with a small wooden cross.

9

Will Freedom Come in Time?

ON 22 January 1945 another batch of letters arrived in the camp—but many of the prisoners still didn't receive any. On 8 February the Australian Sisters had their first fatal casualty, Sister Ray Raymont. She was the Sister whom Netta Smith described as having been made to stand in the sun for some trivial offence—and she had never recovered from the ordeal. Her death was followed shortly by that of Sister Rene Singleton of the 2/10th Australian General Hospital; she was in her early thirties. A few weeks later Sister Blanche Hampsted of 2/13th AGH, a Queenslander, died of malnutrition and beri-beri after a long illness in hospital. The Australian Sisters—who had remained throughout a strong and cohesive body and a great source of strength to their fellow internees—were now reduced to twenty-nine. Then, in March, Commandant Siki

196

announced that the prisoners were to be moved to a place called Loebok Linggau on the southern side of Sumatra.

Margot Turner takes up the story:

We were told that we were to go back across the Banka Strait, sixty miles up that hateful river to Palembang, then by train across Sumatra and finally in trucks. Our first feelings were, thank God we are going to get away from this ghastly camp, with its deadly fever and mounting deaths. Anything would be preferable to this. But we little knew what the journey would prove to be like. Just before the move started the Australians lost another Sister, Shirley Gardham from Tasmania, of the 2/4th Casualty Clearing Station. She just fell down and died in a matter of minutes.

The move started on 8 April 1945, when the first of three groups went off. This was the worst journey of all because so many of the people were now so weak and ill and several died on the way. We left the camp in open trucks in the pouring rain and were driven at break-neck speed to the pier, where the stretcher

197

patients were unloaded and put on the grass under the trees. One Dutch woman died there and her body was put in a lorry going back to Muntok. She was the last of our prisoners to be buried in the little Chinese cemetery among the wild flowers.

Those who could walk started off, carrying their own baggage, along that interminably long pier. The more active people, chiefly the Sisters, had to act as stretcher-bearers, going up and down that pier many times, carrying and helping those who were too ill to walk. There was a big difference in the pier since I had seen it last. Now there were gun emplacements every few yards and Japanese soldiers everywhere. They gave no help to the sick and weary file of women who staggered past them.

It took some hours to muster all the party at the end of the pier. And then the stretcher patients had to be got on board a launch—which was bouncing about in the water—while the remainder of us had to go in an old wooden cargo vessel. We were crowded like sardines on the decks, women and children together, without room to lie down or stretch our legs. The rain had ceased and it was scorching hot.

Many of the women and children had dysentery. The Dutch nuns managed to get some bedpans and we Sisters had to do our best with these. To empty and clean the pans we had to lower them with ropes into the sea and drag them up again. This was an absolutely killing job.

Before starting a young Englishwoman died and was buried at sea. That night, anchored in the mouth of the Moesi River, was bitterly cold. At dawn we started up the river—for the third time —and arrived at Palembang some time in the afternoon. It had taken us twenty-six hours in that awful old ship and everyone was burnt black by the sun. Out of the three parties eight people had died on the voyage and were buried at sea.

When we had disembarked on the wharf the Japs insisted on having a "Tenko". This was an interminable business as they couldn't get the figures right and we had to explain about those who had died on the way. At last we were given a drink; and this saved our lives.

Then followed the rail journey, the

stretcher patients being put into cattle trucks and the rest of us in carriages. This was certainly better than the blazing sun but we had to sit there in the siding all night; and the Japs insisted that all the doors and windows should be closed and that there should be no lights. Six of the patients in the cattle trucks died during the night. However, during the night we got a meal of what the Japs called "bread". It was heavy, hard and tough, but it was a great improvement on the rice.

Early next morning the train started and we were allowed to raise the blinds to get some fresh air, although we had to pull them down at every station: the Japanese mentality was always hard to fathom. But we managed to buy a few pineapples and bananas en route.

We arrived at Loebok Linggau at 8 p.m. and hoped to be allowed out of the train to stretch our legs and get some fresh air; but we were made to spend the night once more in the carriages and trucks. For three nights running we all had to sit up and were nearly dead with weariness, thirst and hunger; and we Sisters were more weary than most as we had to give what help we could to the sick.

Just before dawn we were herded out of the carriages, the Japs swinging their bayonets round our legs to hurry us along. The stretcher cases looked in very bad shape and several more had died. Many of the others had to go into hospital on arrival.

A few hours later we were bundled into trucks and taken to a rubber plantation which, in pre-war days, had been one of the largest in Sumatra. Everywhere there was broken machinery and it was obvious that the owners had carried out their "scorched earth" instructions most thoroughly. The whole place looked an absolute wilderness. The four days' journey had been hell and again much of the luggage of the stretcher cases had been looted or lost.

Our new camp was in the middle of the rubber estate and the accommodation was large, consisting of badly built attap huts with leaking roofs and sides and mud floors. The huts were on a hill on the far side of the creek from the hospital. On the flat side of the creek was the lower camp, where the British and Dutch kitchen staff lived close alongside the community kitchen. Past the kitchen block was a one-roomed cottage with a balcony, where the eighteen Charitas nuns lived. Next door there was a smaller one-roomed hut which accommodated ten Australian Sisters. These nuns and nurses were the hospital staff. The remaining Australian Sisters lived on the hill at the top of the camp. There were about six hundred people living up there and they had to carry up the hill every drop of water they wanted from the creek. There were boards instead of branches to lie on, which were more comfortable—but the huts were full of bugs and rats. Each person had twenty-two inches of bed space. There were no bathrooms; bathing was in the stream—in full view of the Jap guards and the Hey-hoes. Except for this the bathing facilities were good and we could have a complete wash in cold running water.

It was on this last journey that Mary Cooper, who had been a stretcher case, became very ill with beri-beri. The Japs told her on arrival that, as she was Irish, she could leave the camp when she got better, and they gave her some injections. She was terrified at having to go—and very rightly so as her fate would have been unpleasant. But the matter didn't arise as death intervened.

In our last camp we had missed having the male internees near us. Now we found their camp was quite close; but no contacts were allowed. However, it was a support—particularly for women who had husbands or sons interned—to know that they were near us.

Soon after we arrived in the new camp our dear Miss Dryburgh died. She had been sick for some time and the move from Muntok had been too much for her. Her death cast a gloom over the whole camp. However, a big batch of mail had now arrived, all the letters dated 1942 or 1943.

The 8th of May 1945. If only the prisoners could have known that Germany had surrendered unconditionally on the previous day and all hostilities on the western front had ceased; and that later in the same month Rangoon was to fall to General Slim's victorious 14th Army. What a lot of lives these momentous tidings might have saved in the women's camp.

The women were soon to confirm from their own bitter experience that Loebok Linggau was notorious all over the Indies for the virulence of its malaria. And a large proportion of the prisoners were now suffering from beri-beri as well.

Margot continues her story:

Soon we were up against the eternal problem of food, how to cook it and how to supplement it. The rice ration was reduced and we got sweet potatoes, carrots, bringals and beans. This made a change and all sorts of ways of cooking them were tried, with varying degrees of success. We supplemented the ration by cultivating small gardens. Twice meat was issued; on each occasion it was a piece weighing five pounds—to feed six hundred and forty people. But the cooking and issuing of food proved increasingly difficult in this camp as the inmates got weaker. It was too long a carry from the kitchens up the hill and supplementary cooking arrangements had to be made, which were not very satisfactory; and the carrying of the water became an increasingly intolerable burden.

Suddenly, to our amazement, we were told on 15 May that a Jap military band would entertain us. We thought that something must have happened for them to make such a gesture. We were not very keen to hear the band and not many people went; so the Japs more or less chased us up at the point of the bayonet. Actually it was a great success. There were about thirty Japs in the band and they played good music and played it well. it was mostly German music, waltzes and overtures that we knew. One Japanese sang—and very well. The concert took place in beautiful surroundings and we all sat in the shade of some rubber trees. Next day we were all told we had to write and thank the band and say how much we had enjoyed it.

However, life continued to be very hard. Out of sheer weakness scores of the prisoners died in the camp in these last months of captivity. Many of the children were in a terrible condition, some of them so badly affected by beri-beri that they could hardly walk. The hospital was full and the Sisters found it very hard work. Malnutrition was making itself felt to an increasing extent. Quite a lot of time had to be spent in making patients eat. We would sit for hours trying to make them take even half a teaspoonful every five minutes. If they refused to eat at all they very soon died. It was very grim and exhausting nursing—particularly as some of us Sisters were in need of nursing ourselves. On the long wooden benches in the hospital, which served as beds, the patients lay cheek by jowl. It was quite impossible to separate the dysentery cases, or any other cases, and survival was largely a matter of luck.

On 31 May another nursing Sister died. She was Gladys Hughes of 2/13th AGH of Victoria, a New Zealander. The Australians were to lose three more Sisters before the end.

The supply of wood became a greater problem than ever. All the rice had to be cooked by ten o'clock in the morning in the community kitchen and then issued to the various blocks. The rice had to be reheated for the mid-day meal and the evening meal in the little local kitchen in each block. Dead branches and dead trees were precious windfalls but we were not allowed to get the dead rubber trees outside the camp. The Japs still seemed to want to make everything as difficult and exhausting as ever. "Tenko" now took place twice a day, which was a great nuisance. However, we were now getting an increased issue of red palm-oil—which we had only obtained previously in very small quantities—and we could use it for lighting in the huts. This was a great help to us in getting into our mosquito nets and also for those unfortunates who had to find their way to the latrines, perhaps several times during the night.

July came, and although there were rumours that the war was nearing its end, which came from certain Dutch and Eurasian women who had been over-friendly with the Japanese guards, there was no let-up in the camp restrictions.No communication whatever was allowed between the two camps, which was particularly hard on the Dutch, where there were relatives in both camps. Early in July another batch of cables and letters arrived, mostly for the Australians, and dated 1943 and 1944. The Japs, of course were severe censors but they had let one thing pass, almost certainly because they did not understand its significance. Some of the recent letters from Australia had mentioned that so-and-so had been "demobbed". Could it mean that the war was over?

The first indication of any change of attitude on the part of the camp guards came on 20 August, when the prisoners were given fourteen live pigs. Every possible edible part of all of them, including the ears and tails, was made into one huge stew in the community kitchen. The people who could still manage to digest it certainly had one satisfying meal.

Before the end of the month there were only twenty-four Australian Sisters remaining out of the sixty-five who had left Singapore in February 1942.

Netta Smith writes, "Had we been kept in the camp much longer Margot would have had a breakdown—she had worked herself to the bone and was sick in hospital with fever. What a wonderful person she was and what a splendid example she had set."

It was on 6 and 9 August that the two atom bombs were dropped on Hiroshima and Nagasaki and Japan had surrendered unconditionally on 14 August. Whatever may have been said in after years about the dropping of these bombs it certainly saved the lives of thousands and thousands of American and British Servicemen and also of the prisoners of war of the Japanese, both military and civilian. But the prisoners in the camp at Loebok Linggau heard nothing about the end of the war until twelve days later—twelve days in which many of their lives hung in the balance and in which some succumbed.

On 20 August they were inspected by a high-ranking Japanese official and made to stand at attention and bow as usual; but shortly afterwards the Camp Commandant told them that all the children in the women's camp could visit their relatives in the men's camp—about a mile away. Only children under twelve were allowed to go; but some could not walk the distance owing to sickness and malnutrition and some were too young. The children born in internment were now only three years old.

But what tremendous excitement there

was. The mothers dressed up the children as well as they could and tied their hair in ribbons if they still had any. They all assembled at the guardroom, where their names were listed. The Japs then called out the names of the children who couldn't go. In some cases this was the first indication that they and their mothers had had that the fathers or brothers were dead, some of them more than a year previously. And some of the children had to give the sad news of the deaths of their mothers.

When the children returned they had wonderful stories to tell of how their fathers looked and they were laden with notes, parcels, sweets and fruit. Next day Commandant Siki ordered that all children whose mothers had died but whose fathers still survived were to move over permanently to the men's quarters. As some of the children were now quite young women this seemed stranger than usual, even by Japanese standards. But although *they* knew the war was over they wouldn't allow husbands and wives to meet.

By now, however, there were increasingly strong rumours in the camps that the war was indeed ended and at last, on the afternoon of 26 August, Commandant Siki summoned all the prisoners to a meeting. "War is over," he told them. "Americans and British will be here in a few days. Now we are all friends."

What rejoicing there was among the prisoners. No more "Tenko", no more irksome restrictions, no more bullying—and best of all no more bowing to the superior race. Hope had not been in vain and soon they would be free—to be clean, to eat normal food, to wear proper clothes, and, at last, they would be free from the terrible manual labour which had been the cause of so many deaths.

The glad news was taken to Margot and the other patients in the hospital. There couldn't have been a better tonic. And at once the medical supplies which they had needed so badly and which had been denied them so long, came pouring into the hospital from the guardroom—bandages, quinine, vitamin tablets, powdered milk, butter, huge mosquito nets and every other sort of comfort. These must of course have come from the Red Cross parcels which the Japanese were now frightened of using themselves.

Margot recalls:

What really brought home our freedom to us was the arrival of the men from their camp to see their families and also to help us with some of the heavy camp work which still had to go on. There were very few of the British men left alive but it was a very joyous occasion all the same. And the Japs had actually issued us with a lipstick for every two women, so we tried to look a bit more presentable. The men couldn't do enough for us. They went into the jungle and shot wild pigs and deer and, what with one thing and another, we were soon getting more food than we could eat. But perhaps the most welcome thing of all was soap—which we had hardly seen for three years.

The extra proteins in the diet and the exciting prospect of release were making me feel stronger every day. Netta Smith, though now only five and a half stone in weight, had kept amazingly fit—chiefly because of her indomitable spirit.

The men continued to come over every day to cut the firewood, carry the water, do the cooking and give us all a chance to recover our strength. The meat, the butter and the milk were doing wonders for us; but the waiting became more and more irksome and we began to think that no one knew where we were and that we might be left in the camp for years. Even now we hadn't heard any firm news of what was happening in the outside world and only discovered afterwards that General MacArthur had invited the United States' General Wainwright—who had been the American commander in the Philippines when they had surrendered in 1942—and General Percival, to be with him when he took the surrender of the Japanese on the United States battleship *Missouri* in Tokyo Bay on Sunday 2 September 1945. The next day Wainwright and Percival flew to Manila in the Philippines for another surrender ceremony which took place on 3 September. There, General Percival met his old opponent, General Yamashita, to whom he had surrendered the Allied Army in Malaya on 15 February 1942. Yamashita was later executed for the crimes against humanity committed by his troops.

On 10 September General Percival arrived home at Swindon aerodrome, where he was met by his wife, Betty—who never really recovered from the anxieties she had undergone over her husband's defeat and captivity. It may be coincidence but what a lot of the prisoners' wives died prematurely after their husbands' return. And when one considers the terrible burden of anxiety they had to bear, bringing up their children on a tiny pittance, and hiding their fears as best they could, no widow's allowance for them and no way of planning for a future which was without very much hope, it is not really surprising that at long last some of them cracked.

Margot continues her tale:

The Japs were now sending more and more comforts into the camp every day —medicines, for lack of which our friends had died; mattresses, which would have relieved us of infinite discomfort—particularly in the hospital—and Japanese tinned meat, which could have saved many a death from malnutrition. And for the first time since we left Singapore we got an issue of butter. We also received an issue of Japanese clothing, some of which—particularly footwear, which we hadn't had for ages—was useful. But we wisely took it all and used what we didn't want to sell on the black market for fresh food.

Our fears about being forgotten were set at rest when a South African dropped by parachute. He told us that they knew roughly where our camp was but had had difficulty in finding us. During the second week in September another plane flew over, dropping fresh bread and medical supplies by parachute; and then, late on 17 September, the Australian Sisters got a message to say that an Australian plane was landing early next morning and would take off the Australian Sisters and the very sick British. There was acute depression when they had gone. The Dutch of course had all gone by now and we were left alone.

However, twenty-four hours later another aircraft arrived at Lahat in which Netta and I were both taken. We went from the camp as we had come—in Japanese open trucks. We had the same Japanese truck drivers who had been so insolent to us when we had arrived; now they were offering us sweets and butter wouldn't have melted in their mouths. On the train journey to Lahat the Japs, who had treated us like cattle before, were coming round with curry, but we had brought our own rations and had the satisfaction of refusing their offers.

What a thrill it was when we arrived at the little aerodrome and saw the aircraft, which was to take us back to liberty and civilization, appearing over the hills and then landing. It was my first experience of air travel and not the most comfortable as there were no seats and we all sat on the floor. But what did anything matter except that we were leaving a hateful place and a terrible experience behind. We arrived in Singapore on 19 September.

Meanwhile in Changi Camp on Singapore Island the condition of many of the military prisoners was becoming parlous owing to the brutality and neglect of their captors. Every now and then a near-corpse would be delivered to the camp from Outram Road Jail. Many prisoners had been allowed to rot and die in that prison and now these odd moribund bodies were sent back to Changi —often too ill to be saved. Rations had begun to decline steadily until, in July 1945, the average ration totalled eight ounces of rice a day and less than half an ounce of fried fish, with a few ounces of green vegetables and tapioca root grown in the camp gardens. The Japs continued their policy of under-feeding the sick, and men in hospital dragged out an existence that could only lead ultimately to death.

The urgent question was how long would their sufferings last and how much suffering could they take? The general decline in weight alarmed the British doctors and even men fit enough to do heavy work looked like walking skeletons. They did, however, have one morale-raiser denied to the women's camps: they had a concealed wireless set which gave a regular and truly wonderful information service throughout the camp. They had, of course, the advantage of trained signalmen to run it and during the whole of their captivity they had received extracts from the news bulletins from London, New Delhi and America and heard parts of Winston Churchill's speeches, comments by Wickham Steed, and many even received messages which gave them news of the safe arrival home of their families. This service continued for the best part of two years, surviving many Japanese searchings and dire warnings of execution by the dreaded Kempei Tai. Discovery would have meant torture first to obtain information of their confederates—and then certain death.

In August the prisoners in Changi knew that the end was at hand. They heard on their radio the Emperor's announcement that the Japanese Forces were to lay down their arms in unconditional surrender. Nevertheless, the Japanese guards continued to say nothing and the prisoners had to pretend that they in their turn knew nothing either. Then at last the news was officially announced and that afternoon a large party just walked out of the camp and went for a bathe in the sea—and as they passed, the Japanese camp guard turned out and presented arms! That evening a doctor in the Royal Army Medical Corps and an infantry officer parachuted into Changi airfield—and they seemed to the gaunt and haggard prisoners like people from another world, with their round faces and muscular physique.

The next morning a woman, the head of an ENSA concert party, came into the camp. She was the first woman they had seen for three years and they clustered round her as though she was something from Madame Tussaud's and might melt away before their very eyes.

The prisoners then walked out, with their small bundles of worldly possessions tied up in blankets—and went to find lodgings in Singapore.

So ended a terrible time in the lives of the British prisoners of the Japanese. The military prisoners had undoubtedly had the worst of it; but they were run pretty close by the sufferings of the women. It says much for the mental and physical resilience of these people that many of them recovered and were able to lead a normal life thereafter; but many were not.

10

Home At Last

DENIS RUSSELL-ROBERTS and the other British officers of the 5/11th Sikhs had a very touching and joyous reunion with their Indian soldiers, hideously thin and many of them desperately ill. Most of them had been brainwashed and tortured in an endeavour to make them forswear their British allegiance and join the Japanese-sponsored Indian National Army. Several of them had been put to death to persuade the others to give in. Separation from their British officers, in whom they placed such implicit trust and confidence, had a great moral significance as far as the Indian ranks were concerned and it is not to be wondered at that, under extreme mental and physical pressure, a number of them gave in. It is to their underlying credit that the great majority resisted—and the Gurkhas, most of whom had been captured in Burma in the first few months of 1942, resisted to a man.

A few days later the British and Indian prisoners were visited by the "Supremo", Admiral Lord Louis Mountbatten. Lady Louis was following him closely down the line, looking very smart in the uniform of the St. John Ambulance Brigade. Denis Russell-Roberts told her that his wife, Ruth, was a prisoner in the women's camp in Sumatra and she said that she would make arrangements for him to be flown over there as soon as possible. On the next day, however, he was informed that all the women and children who were in prison camps in Sumatra were being flown back to Singapore. But for Denis the weeks of waiting, after all these years, were almost the hardest to bear. Nearly three weeks had passed since they walked out of Changi Camp and nearly all his friends had left by ship for India. Only three of the British officers remained in Singapore.

On 19 September Denis witnessed the Japanese surrender to Lord Louis Mountbatten. Six days later he received a message telling him to go to Alexandra Hospital where a large batch of women prisoners from Sumatra was due to arrive at any minute.

He stood in the hall of the hospital as they got out of the lorries and walked up the entrance steps. How ill and weary they looked, unkempt, haggard and thin as rails. Then he saw Christine Bundy—alone—and no Ruth. Suddenly he felt a fierce stab of anxiety. Christine saw him and at once came over to him. She just squeezed his hand and whispered: "So sorry, Denis."

Next morning, when Denis had recovered a little, he went back to the hospital and heard from Christine the sad details of Ruth's death. He also had a long talk with Vivian Bullwinkel and heard all her terrible story. The experience of Denis Russell-Roberts was one of many tragedies at this time; but it was a particularly sad and dramatic one. Denis and Ruth had been very much in love and had both so very nearly survived to be reunited.

During the following day many telegrams were sent from Singapore, giving good tidings, or bad tidings—or no tidings at all—to anxious relatives at home. Many of those who had been reported missing, believed prisoners, had in fact been killed or died without being taken prisoner at all; and the lot of their relatives—who had hoped against hope all the weary war years—was perhaps the hardest to bear.

Margot Turner and Netta Smith and the others who were with them, arrived on the following day and were sent straight to the luxury of Raffles Hotel. Netta called at the Hong Kong and Shanghai Bank and was surprised and delighted to find that her 600 dollars credit was still there. All the next week they revelled in the luxuries of civilized life—as many baths as they wanted, silk and cotton underclothes and pyjamas, good food—though here they had to be very careful not to eat too much—and a nice long whisky and soda, or even two, in the evening.

Then, on 26 September, Margot and Netta, together with several of their friends from the camp, sailed for England on the Polish ship *Sobieski*. There were fifteen hundred men on board and only ten women, amongst whom were Dr. Margaret Thompson, two nurses from the Malayan Nursing Service, Mary McCullum from Dundee, Bunty Copeland, a teacher, and a very attractive Eurasian girl, Olive Bayliss, married to a British Army Sergeant, who was going home to make the first acquaintance of her in-laws—and of England. Her husband was missing and she had no idea whether he was alive or dead. Margot Turner was the only QA on board. Margot recalls:

The ship was very comfortable. We were treated with the greatest care and not given any rich food. On the ration was a free whisky and soda every night. We stopped off at Colombo, where we were issued with some Red Cross clothing. We had started to recover during our week in Raffles Hotel and we continued the process on the voyage.

We had a lot of news to catch up with. We didn't know what had happened in the war after the fall of Singapore. We didn't know that there had been a General Election and were shocked to hear that Winston Churchill was no longer Prime Minister. We went ashore at Port Said and the civilian nurses were issued with a whole heap of clothing. Netta got a pink flannelette nightdress, which was a present from the Mayor of Boston, USA, and which she wore at the fancy dress dance when we got back on the ship.

At long last, on 24 October, after nearly a month's voyage, we arrived at Liverpool. There Netta Smith and I parted company, which was rather a sad parting after all the harrowing life-and-death experiences we had been through together. Netta went back to her job in Malaya in 1946 and stayed there until 1961. I saw her again when I was posted to Hong Kong in 1960 and we have always kept in touch and remained friends.

On arrival at Liverpool all the military personnel had to go to the transit camp for the night to have a brief medical inspection. Next day we went in a special train to London. The train went into every siding possible, which was very frustrating as we could hardly wait to get to London to see our families. We left Liverpool at 11 a.m. and didn't arrive at Euston until 7 p.m. All that was special about the train was that it was specially slow.

Margot was given six weeks' leave and went straight to her mother at Hove. Her old friend, Nancy Sutton, had kept in close touch with Margot's mother throughout the war. Margot had been posted as missing and there had been no definite news of her being alive until her mother got her cable from Singapore. Nancy had been invited down to Hove to welcome her friend on her arrival; she says, "Margot was very thin and yellow-looking and had some of her front teeth missing. But she was mentally very cheerful."

Actually Margot had had one front tooth knocked out by a Japanese soldier and, just before the end of their imprisonment, she had an abscess in another one, which had to be removed when she arrived in Singapore. She was also rather lame from a large log having fallen on her foot in the camp, which had probably broken a bone. She found wearing shoes both difficult and painful for some time.

But there was no doubt that Margot's old spirit and will to live were still burning like a bright flame and she was determined to face the future with the same courage and determination she had shown in facing the past.

11

Facing the Future

RETURNED prisoners of the Japanese were in a particular category. They had not only been physically and mentally maltreated as no other prisoners of war had been—deliberately starved of food and essential medicines in a tropical climate—but they had been starved of news from their loved ones who, in most cases, didn't know if they were alive or dead. And many of the wives at home had given up hope of ever seeing their husbands again. The people in Britain, however, did at least know how the war was going and that, after the first bad years and the bombing, our side was winning! In such conditions the saying that "Absence makes the heart grow fonder" was often sadly awry. I suppose there were more broken marriages among FEPOWs (Far Eastern Prisoners of War) than among any other class of people. And those marriages which did knit up again

227

had to face many painful adjustments, both physical and mental.

For a start most of the FEPOW were suffering from one or other of the many tropical diseases, in addition to malnutrition, from which in many cases it took years to recover. Very few of the military ex-prisoners were accepted for, or desirous of, further service in the Army; and of course many of them had only joined up for the war. Senior officers such as General Percival—despite his high standing and brilliant record before the war—found themselves peremptorily retired. It is to General Percival's eternal credit that he didn't withdraw from life to grow cabbages in the country but gave most of his remaining years to the care of the men who had been fellow prisoners with him; and he was instrumental in building up the Far Eastern Prisoners of War Federation into one of the finest ex-Service associations in the country.

Another man who came back into life in a most valuable way was the Rt. Rev. John Leonard Wilson, Bishop of Singapore, who had been so brutally tortured by the Kempei Tai—and who, in my opinion, might well have been awarded the George Cross.

Though very frail and ill when he was released from captivity, he refused immediate repatriation and stayed on in Singapore to organize relief measures—a task of immense and urgent importance. When he returned to Singapore in 1947 he took Services of Baptism and Confirmation in the Cathedral. Amongst those he baptized and confirmed was one of the men of the Kempei Tai who had been responsible for taking a leading part in his torture. Perhaps it has seldom been given to any one man in modern times to demonstrate his Christian faith in so clear and dramatic a fashion.

To the Far Eastern Prisoners of War, whose Service of Remembrance he takes nearly every year at the Festival Hall, Leonard Wilson—later Bishop of Birmingham and awarded a KCMG in 1968—is a legend and a wonderful example of true Christianity. Always his theme is forgiveness of our enemies—never of bitterness and vindictiveness. Margot shared this Christian feeling. She has remained extraordinarily free of any bitterness towards the Japanese. The Bishop got back into active life after his years in captivity in the best possible way—by going on working at his pre-war job. And that is just what Margot did.

Colonel A. Flanagan, who served later with Margot at the QA Depot and became one of her great friends, recalls her impressions of Margot at the Nursing Association Reunion in 1946:

She was gaunt and showing obvious signs of deprivation from her years in Japanese captivity. But I was struck by her ability to re-adjust to normal life without any bitterness or rancour against the Japanese. To me this was an indication of the courage which had enabled her to survive her many great ordeals since the fall of Singapore.

As time went by I got to know Margot more and more. It was remarkable that, within a short space of time, her behaviour and general attitude to life were such that she might only have been away from England on an ordinary overseas posting!

Indeed Margot did recover from her terrible experiences in a most remarkable way. She had always been a simple and uncomplicated person, although a very strong character. She herself once said, "I don't think about myself very much. I think about what I have to do." So now she put her bitter memories firmly behind her and looked to the future.

Margot was one of a small handful of QAs, who had been prisoners of war, who continued in the Service again afterwards. And it was an amazing triumph that she should have then risen to the very top of her profession. She relates:

When I started my leave I was told that, after it was over, I would have a medical board and then, if I was considered fit enough, I would go back to duty. My leave ended on 10 December and I then got a telegram from the War Office ordering me to report to our Depot, which was at Holmwood in Surrey, subject to my having been passed fit by a medical board.

A board was therefore arranged at once. The Medical Officer was a bit doubtful about my foot and thought perhaps I should have a bit more leave —to which I gladly agreed as I hadn't had a Christmas at home since 1931. In February 1946 I was awarded the MBE —presumably for my war service. I didn't receive it for nearly two years, when I was in Benghazi, and it arrived in the post. There was no citation with it. I also got a Mention in Despatches in February of that year—so I had the MBE, the 1939/45 war medal and the Pacific Star (which was awarded to very few women).

In February 1946, my leave having ended, I joined our holding unit at Anstie Grange in Holmwood, Surrey. I was joined there by three other QAs—who hadn't been with me during the war but who had also been prisoners. We hung about doing nothing at Anstie Grange for three weeks and I became very impatient as I was anxious to get back to work. We were then posted to Shenley for about a month, and in March, we were posted to Horley, where Millbank Hospital had moved after it was bombed out of London. I stayed at Horley as Theatre Sister. In August of that year I was promoted to Senior Sister, which was the equivalent of a captain, and I put up three pips.

Colonel Marsden, the Surgeon at Horley (later Brigadier A. M. Marsden, CBE, FRCS), recalls Margot as follows:

When Margot Turner came to me I already knew something about her POW background, including the terrible privations she had suffered while she was adrift on the sea for some days. I was a bit of a perfectionist in the theatre and a specialist in both general and orthopaedic surgery. When she joined my theatre staff she told me that she had forgotten most of her theatre technique, but I told her that once you have learned to ride a bicycle you can always ride a bicycle, no matter how long you have been away from it. I deliberately plunged her into the deep end as a Theatre Sister opposite me in all varieties of operations, from the relatively minor, for example, hernia, to the major ones, for example, bone grafts, and I deliberately took the attitude that she was an efficient Theatre Sister who knew her job. Certainly there were a number of minor corrections that had to be made, such as recalling to her memory the names of different instruments, but, other than that, provided I worked at a slower pace than usual, she was able to keep up with me, and at the end of a week the atmosphere of being "lost" was quickly replaced by confidence, and she became in a very short time one of the most efficient Theatre Sisters I have ever had.

Perhaps the re-birth of her confidence in herself and in her relationships with the world in general was generated by the handling of her professional duties in the operating theatre.

After Horley, Margot's next posting was to Wheatley, near Oxford. She recalls:

This was purely administrative and I hated not being able to do any nursing. I was then sent on a course at Windsor—nine QAs and thirty WRAC officers. The object of the course was to teach us administration, of which I knew practically nothing. At first I couldn't think what the object was, but later I realized, when we started having to train our own nurses.

After my seven years overseas, however, I was only left in England for eighteen months; and, in May 1947, I was posted to Malta—to the British Military Hospital in Imtarfa. My job was to be a sort of second-in-command to the Matron, although I was not designated Deputy Matron. I had to look after the Mess and relieve Matron of a lot of routine jobs. Our QA ranks had not yet been standardized and I changed mine three times in one year. The Matron was Colonel Rose, a charming person whom I got to know well. But, in December of that year, I was suddenly sent on temporary duty to the British Military Hospital in Benghazi, where the Sister-in-charge had had to go home on urgent leave.

This was the first time I had ever been to Africa. We had half an Italian hospital, which was in the outskirts of the town of Benghazi. Our Mess and Sisters' Quarters were across the road, opposite the hospital, and we had little bungalows with two Sisters in each. The Mess was hutted and the bungalows were brick-built. The hospital was supposed to be hundred-bedded, so we were very understaffed with only twelve Sisters. We had to put extra beds up though as we always had more than a hundred patients, who were all from British troops stationed in Benghazi. There was also a small hospital in Tobruk with three Sisters. We had the ordinary medical and surgical cases, road accidents and normal routine sickness cases that one always gets in a military hospital. We were certainly kept very busy but I found time to play quite a lot of tennis on the court attached to the Mess, and at the Officers' Club. And I started riding again in Benghazi. The horses weren't very good but an Army Riding Club was formed with the local ponies and of course there were plenty of places in which to ride.

Margot was now getting on for thirty-eight and she had recaptured all her enthusiasm for the Nursing Service, in which she had every intention of remaining as long as they would have her. Her fine physique and natural health of body, plus her great strength of character, had enabled her to throw off the effects of her ordeals in the Far East. Moreover, in the various appointments she was filling, in different parts of the world and in different types of hospital, she was accumulating a fund of knowledge and experience which was eventually to lead her to the highest post of all—Matron-in-Chief. But that was as yet a long way ahead.

For the moment, in Benghazi in 1948, Margot took everything as it came and tackled each job with whole-hearted interest and enthusiasm. She had become a famous figure in the QAs, where her war experiences had become well known. But she remained essentially the same person she had always been, liking people, enjoying her many friendships, keen on her sport—of which lawn tennis remained her favourite —and developing her natural powers of leadership all the time. This latter quality is constantly remarked upon by all the people with whom she worked. The quality of leadership and the capacity to make and keep friends often go hand in hand. People liked and trusted Margot. Trust is essential in leadership; and when there is liking too the wheels run more smoothly.

As she had never been to Africa before she found Benghazi and the surrounding country extremely interesting. She visited some of the villages and was invited to an Arab lunch, where she sat on the floor and used her fingers to manipulate a large hunk of mutton. Margot was always curious to know what went on around her. The countryside was very barren. Many of the Italian houses, some of which were quite lovely, had been evacuated when the war started and were housing some Libyan families with their goats and other animals. But already a lot of rebuilding was in progress and, with the discovery of the oil wells, many of the inhabitants had become very wealthy.

Margot recalls:

When I was in Benghazi last, in 1966, there were new roads and new hotels everywhere; the place was hardly recognizable. But in early 1948 there were no Italians and no shops— except the Suk, which was the local market. However, the shops soon started to re-appear.

The QAs were still wearing the traditional grey dress for home service. As the years passed the dress had altered in style and material and had got shorter. But overseas we wore white overalls when on duty and continued to do so until about 1950, when they were replaced by grey dresses of a thinner, semi-tropical material, with short sleeves and no red cape. I think it is very important that a Sister in uniform should look smart and tidy and at the same time be clothed suitably for efficiency at her job. In Benghazi I ordinarily wore the khaki tropical dress, with khaki peaked cap, and when on duty I wore white overalls. Topis had of course entirely disappeared during the war. When I went to India just before the war we always wore a white one with our white hot-weather uniform or a khaki one when we were in khaki uniform, although curiously enough we never wore topis in Malaya.

It is strange, looking back, how important it was considered to be for both soldiers and civilians to wear topis in Eastern countries. When Noel Coward wrote, "Mad dogs and Englishmen go out in the mid-day sun", he didn't even consider the possibility that an Englishman would be *so* mad as to go out without his topi. When I first went out to India in 1912 we not only wore topis but sometimes neck shades at the back and spine pads lower down, in addition to woollen cummerbunds to keep away the deadly stomach chills of evening—all of which gave the soldier such appalling prickly heat that he became more like a mad dog than an Englishman. The young soldiers of the Second World War cast their topis into the dustbin and wore their ordinary service caps. But, early in 1940, in no less a place than Marlborough, topis once more reared their ugly heads. At a highly secret assembly of the brigadiers and commanding officers of 42 Div the huge figure of General "Tiny" Ironside, Chief of the Imperial General Staff, strode into Marlborough Town Hall, with police guarding every door, and told us that we were to be sent to Finland to fight the Russians—and in order to mislead everyone as to where we were really going, we were to be equipped with khaki shorts and topis! What a bit of masterly hallucination. In the end, however, we went to France—so perhaps we double-bluffed someone by not wearing the topis at all!

At the Benghazi Military Hospital Margot was the Sister-in-Charge, which is really equivalent to the Matron. She relates:

We were kept so busy and were so under-staffed that I used occasionally to relieve the Theatre Sister and always made myself on call for the theatre in case of emergency. I rather enjoyed keeping my hand in at a form of work in which I had formerly specialized—before my captivity.

In December 1948 the size of the hospital was doubled from a hundred to two hundred beds, which made it a Major's command—for which I was too junior—and I was therefore posted to Cyprus. I had considerable difficulty in getting there and had to go by air from Benghazi to Port Said, where I caught a ship to Famagusta. My plane was held up in Tobruk and I eventually arrived in Cyprus about a week before Christmas 1948.

The British Military Hospital was in Nicosia. It was a very old hutted building with a large wing for Jewish migrants to Palestine. They were accommodated in an encampment outside Famagusta. The Jewish wing had some of its own nurses, but our Matron and Deputy Matron used to visit it and their surgical cases came to our operating theatre, of which I was in charge when I first went there.

Our Matron was Colonel Somerville and the Deputy Matron, Major Agnes McGeary, was the very famous QA who had accompanied the Chindits in Burma. I remained Theatre Sister for two months; then the Matron was posted home, Major McGeary became Matron and I became Deputy Matron. I was still a Junior Commander with three pips.

In April 1949 I was again detailed for temporary duty in Egypt—at 211 Transit Camp, near Ismailia on Lake Timsah on the Suez Canal. All QAs who were posted to Egypt came through the Transit Camp before joining their various hospitals and all those going home went there too. Although the job was a temporary one I took all my luggage with me as some of these temporary jobs had a habit of becoming very lengthy affairs. Ismailia was certainly a nice place and we had good quarters; but I never liked Egypt or the Egyptians. However, since I had to be there I made the most of it. I went to Cairo, saw the Pyramids and toured up and down the Canal. I was the only QA in the Transit Camp so I was kept fairly busy; but of course the work was entirely administrative.

I was then about to be posted to Salonika; but, as our wing in the Transit Camp was to close in July, it was decided that I should see it through and that another Sister should go to Salonika in my place. So, in July 1949, I was posted for temporary duty in the big Military Hospital at Fayid on the Suez Canal. This hospital had about five hundred beds and at that time there were a lot of British troops in the Canal Zone. We got a number of dysentery cases and some malaria; but I didn't have to do much duty in the wards. I helped the Sister Tutor and the Matron but I also had to continue running the Transit Camp, which had been moved from Ismailia to Fayid, until another Sister took it over.

I was now almost entirely employed on administrative work but, just at that time, a Sergeant in the Argyll and Sutherland Highlanders, who was an ex-POW of the Japanese, had had a bad car accident and was lying seriously ill in a field ambulance at Aqaba. BMH was asked if it could supply a Sister to nurse him and the Principal Matron asked me if I would go. I was delighted at the thought of doing some nursing again and accepted gladly.

I set off immediately for Aqaba in a large plane all to myself and sat with the pilot as we flew across the Sinai Desert. The field ambulance was in tents and they were certainly very pleased to see me. They fitted up a room for me behind the little operating theatre. I was the only Sister there—in fact the only white woman in the place. I nursed the Sergeant for a week until he was well enough to be moved and then I flew back with him to the BMH at Fayid.

In October 1949 I was posted as Matron to the British Military Hospital at Asmara in Eritrea. So once more I took to the air. We came down at Wadi Halfa as there was some trouble with the plane. It was desperately hot. We then flew to Khartoum in the Sudan, where I spent the night in the Sisters' Mess at the BMH, and next morning flew on to Asmara, which is quite high up. I had been in six countries in three years and had now done a great deal of flying. I never liked flying and would always rather travel by sea. I think one has to take to flying when one is young in order to enjoy it and feel comfortable in the air. However, I was obviously going to have a lot more air travel so I made myself become reconciled to it—though I still never fly from choice.

This last remark is typical of Margot's attitude to life. Just as in the prison camp she had forced herself to like rice because there was little else to eat, so now she made herself tolerate flying. Whatever *had* to be done Margot *did* it. She had a great natural acceptance of the inevitable; indeed it was almost a philosophy of life with her.

Margot describes the hospital at Asmara as

. . . small and located in what had been an Italian clinic, which the Army had taken over some three years earlier. Our Mess was in a lovely old house in very nice grounds, which one of the German Generals had had as his headquarters. It had its own private chapel. The hospital was situated quite high up and it was coolish at night and a very pleasant temperature during the day. There were only six QAs there.

Occasionally there were outbreaks of violence between the Italians and the Eritreans and we sometimes had curfews and were confined to our quarters; and we were never allowed to go far from the hospital without an armed escort while I was there. But I managed to get down to the coast for a visit to a place called Massawa, which was very hot but had lovely bathing. I also played a lot of tennis, often with the civilians in the neighbourhood, as we had courts close to our quarters.

I was due for home in May 1950; but they wanted me to go in March. As there was only one ship leaving a month I had very short notice. My heavy luggage had only just arrived from Egypt and I had just unpacked it when my sailing orders came—and I was off once more. Of my first thirteen years in the Army I had done ten overseas.

I much enjoyed the sea voyage home as a pleasant change from constant air travel and on arrival was given disembarkation leave. I went home to my mother and stepfather at Hove. My mother had not been at all pleased that I had only been allowed eighteen months in England after the war and was delighted to have me back. However, in the middle of my disembarkation leave I was sent on a course at our Depot, which was then at Hindhead in Surrey. Having done the course and finished my leave I was posted back to the Depot and, as by that time we had officially been given men's Army rank, I became a Major.

12

A Much-travelled Person

BY 1947 it had become apparent that some form of basic military training would be required by the nursing officers of the future. Accordingly the Depot at Anstie Grange had been opened for this purpose. Here officers were given instruction in such matters as Army organization, drill and administration.

In 1948 Queen Mary became Commandant-in-Chief and a Controller Commandant was appointed. Then, on 1 February 1949, the Queen Alexandra's Imperial Military Nursing Service was given the name by which it is known today—Queen Alexandra's Royal Army Nursing Corps, the change from Service to Corps indicating full incorporation into the Regular Army. Nursing officers were granted regular commissions and, in 1950, were given the same rank titles as male officers.

With the introduction of the Other Rank element in 1950 and the need to train nurses to the General Nursing Council standards, considerable expansion was necessary and the Anstie Grange establishment was transferred to a new headquarters at Ontario Camp, Hindhead, which gave it far greater scope.

The official opening of the Depot, following a brief sojourn at Keogh Barracks in Mytchett, took place on 13 September 1950, a few months after Major Margot Turner had arrived there. The opening was the last public duty of Adjutant-General Sir James Steele, GCB, KBE, DSO, MC, LLD.

Margot found herself appointed as the officer in charge of the parade, which consisted of QAs and RAMC. Margot had to mug up her drill and she was so taken up with this that she forgot to learn how to dismiss a parade—but she managed to get away with it. In his address Sir James remarked that he had never before taken a parade of both men and women which was commanded by a woman.

During the ensuing five years the work of the Depot was firstly, to provide basic military training to newly joined officers and other ranks, and secondly, to provide promotion courses for other serving officers and Other Ranks of the Corps. The syllabus of nurse training was agreed by the General Nursing Council, which had duly recognized that the Army provided the necessary facilities and opportunities for the training of nurses for State Registration.

In 1955 the opportunity to acquire still better accommodation for the preliminary training section arose with the adaptation of the former Isolation Hospital at Stanhope Lines, Aldershot, to a Preliminary Nurse Training School.

When Margot was first posted to the Depot at Hindhead it was decided that she would be made a "Quarter-Mistress", a curious-sounding and unique appointment. She therefore did an attachment to an RAMC Quartermaster to learn all about the job. However, it was then decided that she was too senior and that it wasn't really a job for a QA in any case. So, although she never acquired the unique distinction of becoming the first QA Quarter-Mistress, she found the knowledge she had gained in preparing for the job very useful in after years.

Like many other branches of the Armed

Forces in the years immediately following the war the newly formed QARANC was feeling its way into the post-war scene gradually, sometimes painfully; it was necessary to reduce wartime establishments and yet fulfil obligations to the Army, which was still scattered over many parts of the world. As was the case with the other Services at that particular period, recruiting of staff and nurses was not as good as it might have been.

QAs with the experience and ability of Major Margot Turner were rather few and far between. She was now appointed an Instructor to the Officers Courses at Hindhead—and then was made a Company Commander. Margot recalls:

Hindhead was a large hutted camp. There was no nursing; it was all teaching and administration. We had a staff of fifteen to twenty officers, which varied in strength in accordance with the number and type of courses with which we had to deal. The courses were: Junior, Senior and Territorial Army, and all new Sisters coming into the Corps as young lieutenants would come in for a three-weeks' course to learn their basic duties. All those going overseas came through the Depot and were kitted out with their tropical clothing and dispatched by the Depot to whatever ship or plane they were catching. That is all changed now and they go direct from their units. We had a holding and a drafting section.

Mary Jo Scannell (now Mrs. R. G. Davies) writes of this time:

I first met Margot Turner in early 1950, when I was an Instructor at the QA Depot. She was on a four weeks' Senior Officers' course prior to being posted as our first trainee Quartermaster—an appointment that never materialized— and she became a Company Commander. From that time a friendship started between us which I hope will last a lifetime. My friend, Anne Flanagan, was also at the Depot as Chief Sister Tutor, and the three of us became great friends, sharing all our joys, troubles and sorrows. It was a godsend to have this relationship which kept us going in the very difficult days during the formation of the Depot—which was something quite new to all of us.

We lived in wooden huts—the only heating being stoves and there was never enough fuel to keep them going. Margot lived in my hut, in the next room to me. Almost every night she went out and hewed wood to supplement the issue. I was amazed at her strength and determination in doing this; but her POW days had taught her to fend for herself—and we were never short of logs in consequence. She was a very practical and mechanically-minded person; she could mend fuses, cope with electric wiring, fix Rawlplugs and put up fixtures. She now comes and shows my husband and me how to fix our towel rails on a "Do-it-yourself" basis.

In our hut Margot kept a wonderful store cupboard of all necessities—soap, toothpaste, tins of food and so forth. When I asked her about it she explained: "Jo, I was once short of everything for a very long time and I don't intend to run short of essentials ever again if I can possibly avoid it."

During her stay at the Depot Margot acquired two possessions which were very dear to her. The first was a small black spaniel dog called Rufus; and the second was an equally small and ancient Austin car, which we christened "The yellow peril". The latter was well known in Hindhead and I think the local police turned a blind eye on some of its temperamental performances. Each Saturday the car took us to Guildford to shop and, with the odd noggin, we always had a slap-up meal on Saturday nights.

Rufus was the apple of Margot's eye and when he got ill with hardpad she nursed him with tremendous devotion and pulled him through although it left him slightly paralysed. Margot had to part with him when she left the Depot as dogs were not allowed in her new Mess. This upset her dreadfully.

Living in the next room to Margot, the walls of which were not particularly sound-proof, I was always intrigued to hear her muttering at great length every Sunday afternoon. I realized it was Margot writing her letters; she always spoke as she wrote, a throwback to the grim days of her POW camps, when she spoke her thoughts and couldn't write them down.

We used to pull her leg about this and she took it all in good part.

During our time at the Depot we had the Grand Opening Parade and Drumhead Service. Margot was chosen to be the Parade Commander. None of us knew much about drill, such as was required for an occasion like this, so we had to get down to some very hard practice. This usually took place in a Nissen hut corridor, with Margot marching up and down, receiving and giving commands and perfecting each of the drill movements.

During her stay at the Depot her stepfather, to whom she was very attached, became very ill and Margot went home on every possible occasion to comfort him and help her mother. She never spared herself, regardless of bad weather conditions, and eventually went down with pneumonia and was quite ill in the Cambridge Hospital. Afterwards she was posted to Tidworth and I never soldiered with her again; but we met many times on social and regimental occasions.

Later Margot, Anne Flanagan and I did a motor tour in France together. Margot drove all the way and never turned a hair even when, one day, the clutch slipped on a perilous mountain pass. Whilst we were in France, Anne and I, being Catholics, went to Mass every Sunday and Margot always tried to find a C of E church. Her religion meant a great deal to her.

The qualities I recall particularly in Margot were that she was always meticulous over details and in remembering occasions and incidents. She was never too proud to learn from others and her dealings with people were always fair and generous. She always had nerves of steel and even taught me to drive a car—which was a feat in itself. She *made* me drive, when I thought I couldn't, and she was determined that I could.

Sport has always played a large part in her life. I remember her winning the Medforth Lawn Tennis Cup for the first time. She beat a skilful young player by sheer dogged determination and courage. Her chest was still not clear from her bad go of pneumonia and she got a stitch at times and sometimes was holding her ribs between shots; but she never thought of quitting.

Margot was at Hindhead until 1952, rather longer than intended because, she recalls:

I got pneumonia—probably my war business catching up with me— and was in hospital for some time. I had probably been working too hard and it was decided that I needed a change. I was posted therefore to the large military hospital at Tidworth and put in charge of an officers' ward. Shortly after this I became Deputy Matron. The hospital was part of an old barracks. We had a large number of Sisters and our Mess was part of the Tidworth Officers' Club, which had lovely grass tennis courts. Greatly daring— everyone said I was much too old—I entered for the Medforth Lawn Tennis Cup in 1952, and managed to win, beating a youngster, Captain McConn, in the final.

I was at Tidworth until October 1953, when I was posted to HQ Southern Command, Salisbury, to be an officer under instruction to our Deputy Director of Army Nursing Services—Colonel Morgan. This was my first insight into the higher administration of the Corps. I was still only a Major. I remained at Salisbury for six months, until April 1953, but before that date I was told that I was to be in charge of the QA contingent in the Queen's Coronation.

I was sent from Salisbury to the War Office in London for some specialized training as there was some suggestion that I might be seconded to the Pakistan Nursing Service. I was very glad that this didn't materialize. However, I was kept at the War Office for six weeks to learn what went on there, so far as the Corps was concerned, and I found the experience valuable afterwards.

Margot then went back to the Depot for a month's training and rehearsals for the Coronation. It was certainly a feather in her cap to be selected for this command. The weekend before the Coronation they assembled at the Women's Royal Army Corps camp at Kingston, with the other Women's Services from all over the world. Margot was in charge of the QAs—eight officers and eight junior ranks. Every Corps and Regiment was represented. They had to go round the route and have a rehearsal on the Saturday and Sunday.

On Coronation Day itself they were up at crack of dawn and were taken in coaches from Richmond Park, Kingston, to London. Their starting place was Buckingham Palace and they marched thirteen miles in the procession—Birdcage Walk—Constitution Hill—Hyde Park Corner—through the Park to Marble Arch —along Oxford Street—and then down Regent Street. They spent the whole of a hot summer's day either standing or marching—and at the end they were all quite exhausted. But Margot felt it was one of the most wonderful experiences of her life. And she got a Coronation Medal. After they got back to Kingston it had been arranged that they should return to London in the evening to see the sights; but they were so exhausted that they went straight to bed.

After the Coronation Margot went back to the Depot and won the Medforth Lawn Tennis Cup for the second year running— which proved that there was nothing wrong with her physical fitness.

In July 1953 she was posted to the Royal Victoria Hospital at Netley as Deputy Matron. This was the psychiatric hospital for the Army and at that time it also had some general wards. Margot recalls:

I had never had any experience of, or training for, that side of nursing, but I learnt quite a lot and I found it extremely interesting.

The hospital, standing in beautiful grounds, was of course in a most wonderful position, overlooking Southampton Water. You could see the big ships coming in. I was there until February 1954 when I was posted to Germany and became Matron of the big British Medical Hospital in Hamburg. It had formerly been a German hospital before we took it over. It was a typical German hospital in its lay-out, with a lot of small rooms, which didn't make for convenience from a nursing point of view. However, I thoroughly enjoyed the job. My brother's regiment was stationed just outside Hamburg and my nephew was doing his national service in the regiment, so I saw quite a lot of them both—in fact more than I had ever seen of them during the whole of my QA service.

The British troops much enjoyed being

stationed in Germany as there were all sorts of amenities and splendid facilities for sport and training. There had been a tremendous amount of bomb damage in Hamburg, but it was quite amazing the amount of re-building that had already been done in a short time. I thought Hamburg a very lovely city, with its lake right in the centre and all the shops and sport and pleasure grounds round about it.

As usual Margot took every opportunity of seeing as much as she could of the countries in which she was stationed. And while she was in Hamburg she went to Denmark and spent a long weekend in Copenhagen.

The Hamburg BMH had three hundred beds and took in patients from a wide area—the nearest BMH was in Hanover—and so there was plenty of work. But as Matron Margot didn't do any nursing.

In January 1955 she had an unusual and interesting posting to Bermuda. She recalls this as follows:

When Churchill and Eisenhower met in Bermuda in the latter part of 1953 some British troops were posted back there and it was decided that a small hospital should be set up to look after them. The Medical Specialist, who had been with me in Hamburg, had been sent to Bermuda as Commanding Officer of the hospital and he sent word back to the War Office to say that he would like to have some QAs. So I and a Major Lindsay were flown out there. We spent the first month getting the hospital organized, which was quite a business, and in February we were joined by two more QAs—both lieutenants— one of whom I remember was named Marjorie Smart and the other Thelma (I've forgotten her surname). This small hospital had been built there after the war and then had been closed down. It had only twenty-five beds. The garrison which the hospital now served was a company of troops transferred from Jamaica, a company of the Duke of Cornwall's Light Infantry, and some detachments of REME, Signals and RASC, and we looked after the families as well. It was certainly a very pleasant assignment. The hospital was in a nice situation, overlooking the North Shore. We had a lovely old Colonial-style house for our Mess—just the four of us QAs—and we did a lot of swimming. In fact we spent all our spare time on the beach. It was whilst I was in Bermuda that I got interested in fishing—not that I ever caught anything. I also played a lot of tennis there with the civilians, amongst whom I made a number of friends.

I found Bermuda a most delightful place and I loved every minute of my two years there; but I don't think I would ever want to live there and it does of course get an awful lot of tourists. I joined a woman's club—the Altrusa Club—which was the Bermuda branch of a big American club organization. They had meetings and outings and I met a number of very charming people and was invited to join the Club Committee. It was something quite different from anything I had experienced before as a QA.

I was Matron of the hospital but I also used to help in the operating theatre, which had always been my speciality; and with only one Theatre Sister we were sometimes very short-handed. The Commanding Officer was a physician and there were three other doctors. We could also always call upon the big civil hospital if we wanted an extra doctor or a consultant.

This posting to Bermuda was quite unique and was soon to come to an end so I was determined to make the most of it. I met a very charming American lady, who wasn't married then, and whose name was Miller (later Mrs. Ferguson). She was a registered nurse in America and she invited any of us to pay a visit to the United States. I gladly accepted this invitation and, in September 1956, spent a very pleasant fortnight there, flying to New York and thence to Philadelphia, and staying with Miss Miller in Wilmington, Delaware. I then visited Washington, Philadelphia and New York with her— and also went on a trip to Canada by myself. I travelled in one of those marvellous Greyhound buses right across New York State, Niagara, and on to Toronto, Ottawa, Montreal and Quebec. Then I flew back from Quebec City to New York and from there to Wilmington for Miss Miller's wedding. She married a retired Scottish banker and now lives in Winchelsea in England, where I see quite a lot of them both.

Mrs Ferguson, who came to talk to me about Margot, thinks she is one of the most charming and attractive people she has ever met. As she was a nurse herself, Mrs Ferguson was at once struck by the wonderful way in which Margot, within ten years of the end of the war, had so completely recovered from her ghastly experiences. Although Margot was so dedicated to her profession she had a host of friends and admirers; outside her profession it was among people that her main interests lay. Mrs Ferguson stresses too that Margot was a wonderful friend and says how deeply religious she was—as have so many others. From a professional point of view Mrs Ferguson thinks that Margot's outstanding characteristic was leadership—but by example rather than exhortation. No Senior QA officer could have been more admired and respected by her subordinates —and particularly by the younger QAs.

Mrs Ferguson relates how she and her husband were having breakfast in a hotel in Spain. She happened to say to him: "You must remind me to get a card for Margot Turner." At which a woman sitting a few tables away got up and came over to them.

"Did I hear you say 'Margot Turner'?" she asked.

"Yes indeed."

"Was she in the Queen Alexandra's Nursing Service?"

"She was."

The woman's eyes filled with tears. "She was with my sister in the prison camp when she died," she said, "and she wrote me the most marvellous letter afterwards, telling me all about her. She must be a wonderful woman and I have been longing to meet someone who knew her. Please tell me about her."

Whilst in Bermuda Margot had been awarded the high decoration of RRC (Royal Red Cross), which she received from the Queen at Buckingham Palace in July 1957. Margot recalls that Her Majesty was very interested in her tour in Bermuda and asked her a number of questions about the Nursing Service generally.

Major Turner returned to England in 1957, to take over the appointment of Commandant of the Preliminary Training School at Aldershot. All the nurses or Junior Ranks went there for about six weeks to do their pre-nursing training, as they do in all civilian hospitals—and just as Margot herself had originally done at Bart's. As Commandant she didn't do any of the teaching; her appointment was purely administrative. Nurse tutors gave all the lectures and taught them nursing. It was quite a small establishment—just the Commandant, three nurse tutors and a QA administrative officer.

In April 1959, after two years at Aldershot, Margot was promoted to Lieut.-Colonel and posted as Matron at Millbank where she had been before the war. This, of course, was a very big job. The Commanding Officer was Colonel Llynton Reed, an Australian who was a very fine tennis player of Wimbledon and international standard. Lieut.-Colonel Margot Turner had under her two Deputy Matrons and between twenty and thirty Sisters. There were also a number of nurses in training for their State Registration and Millbank was also a training school for them. Patients came to Millbank from a wide area—and indeed from all over the world.

Colonel (later Major-General) M. H. P. Sayers, OBE, MB—then Editor of the RAMC Journal, who had first met Margot at the BMH Bareilly in 1939—recalls the time that Margot spent at Millbank:

The next occasion I can remember Margot was most dramatic. It was at a Director-General's exercise at the Royal Army Medical College Millbank, in 1959, where a series of lectures were being given before a distinguished gathering of senior British and Allied Medical officers. It was all rather dull until suddenly, to my surprise, Margot took the stage. The atmosphere became charged at once as she proceeded to hold us all spellbound for some twenty minutes with one of the most remarkable stories of the war I had ever heard. It was not only what she said but the way she put it across that gripped us. I doubt if there was a dry eye in her audience and I myself wept unashamedly.

The next time we met was in 1961 when Margot was Matron of the BMH Hong Kong and I remember entertaining her to dinner at the Repulse Bay Hotel which had been one of the last British strongholds before the fall in 1942. Shortly after that she was evacuated through Singapore with trouble in her chest and I remember seeing her while in the BMH there, where I was the pathologist.

Then came the time at the Ministry of Defence, from 1964 to 1967, where I was Director of Army Pathology and she, to everyone's delight, became the Matron-in-Chief.

Describing her time at Millbank, Margot relates:

A lot of senior officers came to Millbank. The hospital was interesting and nearly always busy and I was glad to be back in London again. I had acquired a car—an Austin A30—in Bermuda and I brought it home with me, which enabled me to get out of London when I had a weekend off.

However, her time in England was short-lived. After nearly two years at Millbank she was posted to Hong Kong as Matron of the BMH, the Bowen Road Hospital, and also as Assistant Director of Nursing Services, Hong Kong. She recalls:

I had two jobs. The Bowen Road Hospital was the pre-war hospital and there was also another one which had been built since the war. My foremost job was Matron at the Bowen Road Hospital, but I had to go down to Headquarters occasionally to deal with general matters. Sometimes I visited units out in the New Territories, where we had small Reception Stations. There were a lot of Gurkhas out there as well as British troops. We also had working in the Hospital Chinese nurses and Chinese boys, who were under training. The Chinese were very good and very keen. For the two hospitals there were about thirty British nurses.

I loved Hong Kong, as all Service people used to do. We went racing sometimes; I played golf at a small club at Deepwater Bay—and of course did a lot of swimming. Unfortunately, I wasn't there very long as I had two goes of pneumonia and was sent to Singapore at the end of August 1961 and, after a fortnight there, was sent home to Millbank—this time as a patient.

Even Margot Turner's strong constitution rebelled sometimes against the strain she put upon it and, like most of the ex-POWs of the Japanese, she occasionally suffered from the years that the locust had eaten. However, at Millbank she soon recovered and the specialist said she could go back to Hong Kong. But in the meantime she had been promoted full Colonel, in April 1962, and was sent to Cyprus as DDANS (Deputy Director Army Nursing Service) Near East. Colonel Margot Turner goes on to relate:

My base was at the Headquarters of the Forces in a place called Episcopi. We had a big new hospital at Dhekelia for British troops, on the other side of the island. It was a really splendid hospital and we had a lovely new Mess there. My visits took me all round the Mediterranean—to the BMH in Benghazi, which had moved quite a long way out of the town into new hutted accommodation; to Tripoli and to Malta. But the garrison in Cyprus was being reduced; in Tripoli we were losing a hospital; and in Malta we were giving way to the Navy. By September 1962, only six months after I had been appointed, I had worked myself out of a job. So I was ordered to return home and become DDANS Eastern Command.

My stepfather had died at the end of

1952 and my mother died in February 1956, whilst I was in Bermuda. My eldest brother died of a heart attack in August 1958, aged only fifty-two, whilst I was at Aldershot. So I only had two brothers still living.

I drove home from Cyprus—at least I put my car on a boat as far as Venice and drove from there, with a friend, to Ostend, where I put the car on the little cross-Channel plane.

In September 1962 I went to Hounslow as DDANS Eastern Command, which meant that I was responsible for the nursing in the hospitals of Eastern Command. These consisted of: the Queen Alexandra's Hospital Millbank; The Royal Herbert Hospital Woolwich; the Military Maternity Hospital Woolwich; the Military Hospital Colchester and the Military Hospital Shorncliffe. I was also responsible for the nursing in all the medical units attached to the Command; and I had to attend various committees and boards connected with the Ministry of Defence and officiate at the interviewing of officers who wished to become QAs. I had only been in this appointment eighteen months, however, when I was told, in March 1964, that I was to be appointed Matron-in-Chief and Director of the Army Nursing Service; and I took over from Brigadier Dame Barbara Cozens in July of that year.

13

Matron-in-Chief

IT had been an understood thing in the QARANC for two or three years that there was only one outstanding candidate for the highest appointment in the Corps—and that person was Margot Turner. Her energy and enthusiasm, her experience and her knowledge, her vision and her qualities as a leader—particularly of the young—put her in a class of her own. And her amazing war experiences, the endurance which had brought her through those dreadful times, and the courage that she had shown in putting them behind her, had made her a considerable heroine amongst QAs of all ranks and all ages. Many of them took her as a model and an example. And in October 1964 she was given the honour of becoming a QHNS (Queen's Honorary Nursing Sister).

As Matron-in-Chief Margot was responsible to the Director-General of Army

Medical Services for the nursing in all the British Medical hospitals in the Commonwealth. Her first Director-General was Lieut.-General Sir Harold Knott; and her second, from April 1965, was Lieut.-General Sir Robert Drew.

General Sir Harold Knott wrote on 4 August 1969:

> I am so delighted to hear that you are going to write Dame Margot Turner's life story —and what a story she has to tell! She served under me during my last year in the Chair. As Matron-in-Chief she had all those sterling qualities that one has come to associate with senior members of the QAs.
>
> I met her brother in West Africa; he was a British officer seconded to the King's African Rifles and he fell mortally sick when serving in Tamale. For over a week I never saw anyone nearer death and he surprised me by recovering. He had the same "will to live" as Margot, so it must run in the family.

The Matron-in-Chief was responsible for all the nursing staff and for the nurses in training: and during her four-year tour of office Margot tried to visit hospitals and units at home as frequently as she could. But time and money only allowed her to visit the very distant ones, such as those in the Far East, on one single tour. She also sat on innumerable committees such as those of the Red Cross and St. John's Ambulance Brigade and Associations.

During her second year in office Margot was invited by the Surgeon-General of the United States Medical Corps and the Surgeon General of the Royal Canadian Army Medical Corps to visit the medical units in their two countries. In April 1965 she set out on her memorable tour. She went first to the Pentagon in Washington and met the Surgeon-General of the United States and all his principal officers and was then taken round the famous Walter Reed Hospital. She spent three days going over this vast military hospital of about twelve hundred beds; and she visited another hospital just outside Washington. The Americans showed her the most warm and lavish hospitality wherever she went and were anxious to show her all they could of their magnificent nursing organization. She was asked to give a talk on the history and organization of the

QAs, and was presented with the American Nursing Corps' badge plaque.

Having spent ten days in Washington Margot flew to San Antonio in Texas where she visited the large Brook General Hospital—American nurses do most of their training here, as also do male medical officers and personnel. She spent five days in San Antonio, arriving just in time for a big fiesta where they had wonderful parades of flower-covered vehicles. She then flew to San Francisco, where she spent three or four days visiting many medical units.

Of all the places she visited she loved San Francisco best—perhaps because it reminded her a little of Hong Kong, but on a much vaster scale. She spent a week in San Francisco where she was invited to attend a conference of the National League of Nurses. She also attended a number of meetings and social occasions which she found both enjoyable and interesting.

On Sunday 9 May she flew to Ottawa and spent a week in Canada, visiting hospitals at Ottawa and Kingston, and their Depot and training centre. She would have liked to have seen more of that delightful country but time did not permit.

Margot found the American equipment quite fantastic. Their nursing system and that of the Canadians did, however, differ slightly from the British in that their Sisters do not do so much bedside nursing as English Sisters do and there is therefore not quite the same close relationship between nurse and patient. Also the Canadian nursing organization is not a separate service like the Army Nursing Corps of the United States and the QARANC of Great Britain.

Throughout her arduous tour Margot had been a wonderful ambassadress for the QARANC and established close and cordial relations with the Nursing Services of America and Canada. As always she amazed everyone by her energy and enthusiasm and her determination to make the very most of the wonderful opportunity which had been offered to her.

Soon after her return to England in May 1965 Margot went over to the Continent for the SHAPE Medical Conference in Paris and the International Congress of Nursing at Frankfurt. To Paris she took one of her QA Sisters, Major Rattee, a nurse tutor who was giving a lecture at the Conference. The American General who greeted them said that it was the first time they had had women at the Conference, which was attended by all the Services—Navy, Army and Air Force—of the NATO countries. She stayed at the conference for five days and then went on a tour of the British Military Hospitals in Germany. This involved visits to Berlin, Hanover, Rinteln, Munster and Iserlohn. The last, although a BMH, was a combined hospital in that it had Canadian Medical Officers and Sisters working alongside the British, and large numbers of Canadian patients were taken in.

The International Congress of Nursing at Frankfurt was a civilian affair, which took place every four years. Several of Margot's senior officers in Germany attended. This was the first opportunity she had had of attending this important conference and she was very glad to be able to do so. She stayed there a week and then hastened home to attend to her many pressing duties and engagements.

One of Margot's responsibilities was her Presidency, as Matron-in-Chief, of the QARANC Association, with its Home, Queen Mary's House, for retired QAs. This very nice house at St. Leonard's-on-Sea, near Hastings, had been given to the QAs by Queen Mary and there was always a struggle to raise the necessary finances to keep it going.

In June 1965, in the Birthday Honours, Brigadier Margot Turner received the high honour of Dame of the British Empire (DBE). Although she naturally felt very thrilled—what woman wouldn't?—she felt just a little sad at having to return her MBE, which had been her reward for the dark years when only her will to live had kept her in the land of the living. She felt sad also that her devoted mother, who had always been so proud of her, had not lived to see her so greatly honoured. Margot went to the Palace to receive her DBE from the Queen in July 1965.

At the beginning of November that year Margot went on a tour of the Far East. She first went to Hong Kong, where there were two new hospitals, one of them being the new hospital at Kowloon. She also went all round the New Territories, visiting the medical units and maternity hospitals. From there she flew to Singapore.

Now, in 1965, she found a great transformation. The Alexandra was still the big hospital on Singapore Island, and the Mess was just the same. She went up to the Cameron Highlands by train and passed through Tanjong Malim Station, of which she took a photo. Their old hospital was once more a Malay College. She visited Penang, where there was now a big British hospital; and she also visited the various headquarters and talked to all the senior medical officers.

On Singapore Island the RAF had a hospital at Changi which they invited her to see. She found Changi much changed as there was now a large aerodrome there. She tried to find her old hospital Mess, right on the point, but there was so much rebuilding that she could hardly recognize it. Raffles Hotel was still there but, instead of being the posh hotel of old, it looked dowdy and rather sad compared with the new hotels that had sprung up since.

And so, for the third time in her life, Margot left Singapore—now as Matron-in-Chief and Director of the Army Nursing Service which, in more dangerous times, she had served so gallantly in a much more humble capacity.

In 1966 Margot was busy visiting units

and hospitals in the United Kingdom; but in the spring she paid a visit to Cyprus where, in addition to her own hospitals and units, she was invited to inspect the Royal Air Force hospital at Akrotiri, on the other side of the island. From there she flew to Benghazi. There was no longer a British Military Hospital in Malta; but she went there to see the Assistant Director of Medical Services (ADMS) and tell him her impressions of the hospital at Benghazi. She also inspected the Royal Navy and RAF medical establishments in Malta.

During the year she paid another visit to Germany, again touring the hospitals and seeing the many improvements in the Nursing Service that were being made. Apart from that, however, her visits were confined to the UK.

Mary Jo Davies recalls:

I married Colonel Richard Glanville Davies in 1959 and he was the Commanding Officer at Netley when Margot paid her first visit to the hospital after becoming Matron-in-Chief. Margot also visited us later on when my husband was commanding the BMH at Rinteln in

Germany, and finally once more at Netley towards the end of her tour of office when he was OC there for the second time.

When inspecting a hospital as Matron-in-Chief Margot's main subjects of interest were in the general standards of the hospital, the nursing care of the patients, the welfare of the nursing staff and the training of the Other Rank nurses. She usually spoke to every patient and interviewed any of the nursing officers who had asked to see her. During her visits there was generally a social occasion at which she could meet both the RAMC and QARANC officers informally.

After her retirement my husband and I continued to see Margot frequently. She keeps as active as ever, always has new interests and travels a great deal. But she keeps in constant touch with her old friends, who are always delighted to see her. I remember one amusing occasion when Margot came to stay with us. I had made one of my favourite rice puddings, quite forgetting that Margot had had to live on rice for three years. She ate it quite gracefully—and then said: "That was very nice, but it isn't exactly my favourite sweet"!

Dame Margot's relations with the Chaplain-General and the Royal Army Chaplains' Department were close and friendly. In most of the larger hospitals there was a chapel and an attached chaplain. On several occasions she was a guest at the RACChD's lovely Centre at Bagshot Park. All through British history, from the time of the Crimean War onwards, the doctors, the padres and the nurses have worked closely together in the service of the sick and the wounded.

But it was perhaps in the sphere of training that Dame Margot made her greatest impact during her four years as Matron-in-Chief. She was anxious that the officers should keep themselves up to date with civilian nursing trends. And during her term of office Officer Courses of Instruction at the Training Centre were given a new look, being completely revised, modernized and brought up to date. Margot also widened the scope of the officers' curriculum and gave them opportunities to attend professional courses run by the Royal College of Nursing. This enabled Matrons and Ward Sisters to keep abreast of what was happening in the specialist fields of civilian nursing. She encouraged them to improve their efficiency by being active members of the Association of Hospital Matrons. The value of her advice and opinion was recognized by this Association when they elected her to the Executive Committee of one of their largest groups—a signal honour for herself and her Corps.

So far as the nurses were concerned Margot set firmly on their courses the revised schemes of General Nursing Council training for SRN and SEN, which were adopted in 1964. The planning for this was started several years earlier, but the difficult task of ensuring that hospitals and all grades of nursing staff not only understood the new schemes, but also carried them through, was ably and energetically supported from the top by Margot.

At all times during Margot's tour of office she gave whole-hearted support and wise advice to the Chief Nurse Tutor in her efforts to improve nurse training conditions in Army hospitals. The scope of training had to be widened in order to comply with General Nursing Council requirements and implement the new programmes. Recognition had to be secured from the General Nursing Council for the Army hospitals in which nurses could take the statutory specialist courses. A great deal of forward thinking, coupled with dynamic drive and energy, was required to see these schemes through. And it was in great part due to her initiative and drive that this recognition was obtained and the new programme for nurse training established on a firm basis.

One of the last schemes which Margot saw through to fruition during her term of office was the introduction of Staff Nurse courses for newly qualified nurses, which brought the Corps into line with current trends in civilian hospitals.

During Margot's time as Matron-in-Chief the QARANC Depot moved from its old site in the hutted camp at Hindhead to the new site in Aldershot, where the Royal Pavilion, built in 1856 for Queen Victoria, had formerly stood. Naturally the work of securing this site, and the planning for the buildings and the move, had been started before she assumed office; but the final stages, to ensure that the new Training Centre would prove worthy of the Corps, the smooth working of the move itself, and the arrangements for the very impressive opening ceremony, were the work of Margot.

The foundation stone was laid by the Colonel-in-Chief, HRH Princess Margaret, Countess of Snowdon, CI, GCVO, on 16 May 1963; and the building was formally opened by HRH on 17 October 1967. In February 1968 its title was changed to that of "Training Centre QARANC". It is certainly a most impressive place, standing in beautiful surroundings and it must be an inspiration to those nurses who start their training there.

Dame Margot finished her distinguished four-year tour of office on 26 July 1968 and became Colonel-Commandant of the QARANC in 1969. But her life story as a QA will live on in the memories of many people and in the history of a great Corps, which she served so well.

On Saturday 12 October 1968, the Far Eastern Prisoners of War Federation held their Sixteenth Annual Reunion at the Royal Festival Hall in London. The guests of the evening included the President of the Federation, Brigadier Toosey; the Rt. Rev. J. L. Wilson, Lord Bishop of

Birmingham; Harold Payne, Vice-President; Sir John Smyth, Vice-President; and Brigadier Dame Margot Turner, who was the special guest of the evening.

The Festival Hall was packed with FEPOWs and their families as the Bishop, accompanied by the Rev. John G. Gibson, came on to the stage to conduct the Remembrance Service. The form of the Service has become more or less firmly established over the years. It started with the National Anthem. Then the first prayer:

> We are met together to give thanks to Almighty God for His mercies and to remember before Him those of our number who in the Far East made the Supreme Sacrifice; to pray that God will comfort those who have been bereaved or who are in trouble, and to pray that we may live more worthily for the sake of those who are no longer with us.

Then followed the first hymn, "The Lord's my Shepherd I'll not want". The Last Post. The Prayers. Reveille. The Lesson from Matthew 10, verses 26–33. And then the Address by the Bishop, whose theme, as

always, was forgiveness of our enemies—
and of the future rather than the past.

As I looked at him standing there, with his
grey beard and his flowing robes, I thought
of his tortured body and battered soul,
which not all the brutalities of the Kempei
Tai could subdue. The Bishop will always be
a beloved and saintly figure to the FEPOWs.

The Service finished with the Bishop's
favourite hymn, "The day Thou gavest
Lord is ended". It was followed by the
platform ceremony, conducted by the
supremely efficient Ted Coffey, President of
the London Branch of the FEPOW
Federation. He introduced each of the
"Guests of the Evening". And finally Dame
Margot was introduced and got a warm and
enthusiastic welcome from the vast
assembly of her fellow ex-prisoners of the
Japanese as she stepped forward to make her
short speech. All the lights in the hall were
dimmed except the spotlight which fell upon
her.

She said:

I think the Far Eastern Prisoners of War
Federation is a wonderful organization
because it has brought together many

people who have one thing in common. Being a Prisoner of War of the Japanese has taught us many things, including the real meaning of friendship. The friends we made in those difficult days were true friends indeed and although subsequently our ways may have taken us far apart, we shall always have that one great bond in common. This great assembly here tonight is proof of that.

I am indeed honoured to have been your guest and wish you all a happy Reunion.

As I sat there in the dark I thought back to that burnt and exhausted figure lying on a raft, drifting helplessly and alone in a tropical ocean—and I marvelled again at the strength of the human spirit and the Will To Live.